RENOIR

RENOIR

by

Denis Rouart

SKIRA

RIZZOLI
NEW YORK

© 1985 by Editions d'Art Albert Skira S.A., Geneva

Published in the United States of America in 1985 by
RIZZOLI INTERNATIONAL PUBLICATIONS, INC.
712 Fifth Avenue/New York 10019

Reproduction rights reserved by A.D.A.G.P. and
S.P.A.D.E.M., Paris, and Cosmopress, Geneva

The text by Denis Rouart was first published
in 1954 in the Skira series "The Taste of Our Time"

Library of Congress Cataloging in Publication Data

Rouart, Denis.
  Renoir.

    Translation of: Renoir. Rev. and enl. ed. 1954.
    Bibliography: p.
    Includes index.
    1. Renoir, Auguste, 1841-1919.   I. Title.
ND553.R45T6513   1985   759.4   84-43108
ISBN 0-8478-0585-9

Printed in Switzerland

Contents

C.2

Orchard at Louveciennes: The English Pear Tree, 1875.

Pomona, 1914. Watercolor.

Foreword

A THING of beauty needs no commentary—Renoir himself made this remark and it applies to no other painting so well as to his own. Sufficient unto themselves, his works need no commentary, and it is impossible not to feel a little uneasy as we discuss them, for where can we hope to find the appropriate words—words simple, heartfelt and concrete enough?

If ever an artist stood aloof from theories and ideas, that artist was Renoir. No art is more alien than his to the phrase-making of aestheticians; none is so perfectly attuned to the chords of the senses. We do him violence if, in appraising his works, we lapse into terms even faintly abstract. "Theories don't make a good picture," he said. "Most of the time they only serve to mask an artist's shortcomings. Theories are only worked out afterwards anyhow."

With his instinctive distrust of abstraction, Renoir was led to regard his art as a form of manual labor. "Painting is not a matter of dreaming up or being inspired. It's handicraft first of all and a good craftsman is wanted to do it well," was his opinion. At the same time he expressed his regret that the old apprenticeship system had given way to the academic instruction of the Ecole des Beaux-Arts. All his life he made a point of doing a good job of it, turning out a well-painted picture, with a texture as fine and full-bodied as he could make it. In his last years he grew increasingly concerned with evolving methods of work that would ensure his canvases against deterioration.

Renoir never belittled the headwork that necessarily goes to the making of a work of art. Though perhaps he leaned a little heavily on the idea in order to get his point across, his view was that the mind might suitably be brought to bear on problems which words alone can offer no solution to, but which brushes and pigments can.

And what he thought he carried out in actual practice. Though in the early days he was a familiar figure at the gatherings at the Café Guerbois, he seldom took an active part in the talk, and was not long in showing his true colors. Renoir had a horror not only of art theories, but of all that might encroach on the time he set aside for his work— which, to his mind, was the only way of coming to grips with the real problems of art. "Without actually falling out with them, I have had to break with many good friends. They could never be on time, never go home to bed, and held forth on art far too eloquently. I have no use for that nonsense."

The same distaste came out repeatedly in his conversation. "Don't ask me whether painting ought to be objective or subjective. All I can say is I don't give a damn, one way or the other. I am always bowled over when young painters come to me and blandly inquire what the ends of painting are. Some of them even explain to me why I happened to put on red or blue at such and such a spot on my canvas... Our craft is not an easy one by any means, and I can understand the doubts and anxiety it gives rise to. But after all a little simplicity, a little sincerity!"

His own simplicity and sincerity were as genuine as Corot's, and they are the stuff of his greatness, both as a man and an artist. He rejoiced in being alive, and painting was his way of expressing love of life. The forces within him clamored for fulfillment. And so he painted, with no thought for analyzing the creative act.

Arum and Hothouse Plants, 1864.

Self-Portrait, 1876.

The Early Years

PIERRE-AUGUSTE RENOIR was born at Limoges on February 25, 1841, the next to last of five children. His father, who made a meager living as a tailor, left Limoges in 1845 and moved with his family to Paris. But there he remained as poor as before, and the children were obliged to make their own way at an early age. Pierre was a good-humored, serious-minded boy with a gift for drawing, as the doodlings in his school books prove, and an ear for music that had already impressed Charles Gounod, who was then choir master at the Église Saint-Roch where young Renoir sang on Sundays. There was some hesitation, then, when it came time to settle on a career for him, but in the end his father decided to article the boy to a branch of the ceramics industry, the traditional pride of Limoges. It was hoped that, with his aptitude for drawing, he would develop into a painter on porcelain, a craft that would stand him in good stead for the rest of his life. So at thirteen he entered on his apprenticeship in an atelier of porcelain painters, with the prospect of one day qualifying for a position in the great porcelain factory at Sèvres.

"My job," he later told Vollard, "consisted in sprinkling tiny bouquets on a white ground, for which I was paid at the rate of five sous a dozen. When there was larger ware to decorate, the bouquets were larger too, so that I was paid a little more, but only a little, mind you, since the owner felt that after all, for their own good, of course, he mustn't steep his 'artists' in wealth. All the dishware we painted was shipped off to the Far Eastern countries. I might add that the owner took good care to stamp everything with the Sèvres trademark, borrowed for the occasion. Once I had got into the swing of things, I moved on from the little nosegays to figure painting, but at the same starvation wages. I can remember that Marie-Antoinette's profile used to bring me in eight sous."

Here he learnt to paint with soft, tapering brushes and thin, luminous color. All his life he had a knack of getting a limpidity from colors that played them off against the ground on which they were applied, instead of merely covering it over.

It was now, too, that Renoir's eyes were opened to sculptural form, as a result of visits to the Louvre and the sight of the Fontaine des Innocents. "The factory where I worked," he told Vollard, "was located in the Rue du Temple. I was expected to be there by eight in the morning. At lunchtime, after taking a bite on the run, I used to go over to the Louvre and draw from the antique. One day near Les Halles, as I was scouting about for one of those eating-houses where you can get a cheap hotplate with a glass of wine, I suddenly stopped short in front of the Fontaine des Innocents by Jean Goujon. All idea of the restaurant went out of my mind. I bought a sausage from a nearby butcher and spent my lunch hour inspecting the Fontaine des Innocents. The memory of this experience probably accounts for the special affection I have always felt for Jean Goujon."

Even in his teens, then, his two great loves had taken possession of him: the softly rounded forms of women's bodies and glowing, limpid colors played off against one another.

Portrait of William Sisley, 1864.

Jules Le Cœur in Fontainebleau Forest, 1866.

At the Inn of Mother Anthony, 1866.

At seventeen, with four years of apprenticeship behind him, Renoir saw his plans for the future suddenly go up in smoke. New mechanical processes of reproduction had at last been perfected and the days of porcelain painters were numbered. He had no choice but to look for a new job. "So I began painting fans. God knows how many times I copied *The Embarkation for Cythera*! The first painters I got to know were Watteau, Lancret and Boucher, whose *Bath of Diana* was my first great love. All my life it has held a privileged place in my heart."

This is another lifelong trait of Renoir: his intense delight in all that is happy and smiling in art.

But painting fans brought him no more than a pittance, and he gave it up when he was offered a job painting blinds intended to do duty as stained-glass windows for missionary preachers. The experience he had acquired stood him now in good stead. With his practiced hand he was able to go to work directly on the blind, without squaring up his subject beforehand, as did his colleagues. Since he was paid a set price for each blind turned out, he was soon earning a good living. But to the chagrin of the owner, who even offered to make over the business to him later on if he would stay and make a career of it, Renoir broke away from this drudgery as soon as he had put a little money aside. Taking a few courses at the Ecole des Beaux-Arts (from 1862 to 1864), he enrolled at the same time in Gleyre's studio, where he fell in with Bazille, Sisley and Monet. They could only work up a moderate interest in Gleyre's conventional teachings; but as he was easy-going and tolerant with his pupils, the young men enthusiastically threw themselves into a study of the painters nearest their hearts. Monet turned to Jongkind, Sisley to Corot, and Renoir to Diaz.

Every year when the weather grew fine, the four friends trooped off to Chailly-en-Bière, in the Forest of Fontainebleau, for a spell of open-air painting. The Forest at that time was the haunt of a group of painters who stood aloof from academic circles—the Barbizon School, made up of Millet, Rousseau, Daubigny, Dupré, Troyon and Diaz, often joined by Corot. So it was that Renoir, working alone in the Forest one day, made the acquaintance of the painter he most admired, this in the following circumstances. Taunted by some carefree passers-by because of his porcelain-painter's smock, which, by force of habit, he still wore when working at his easel, Renoir lost his temper. Things were about to take a turn for the worse when an imposing giant of a man arrived on the scene. Despite a wooden leg, he scattered the group of hotheads with a few menacing shakes of his cane. "I'm a painter, too, my name is Diaz," he said, and glancing at Renoir's canvas, he added: "Not badly drawn, but why the devil do you paint so dark?" Advising him to give up using blacks, Diaz opened

Bather with Griffon Terrier, 1870.

Diana (Lise Tréhot), 1867.

The Champs-Elysées during the Paris World's Fair, 1867.

an account for him at his own color dealer's and gave him some useful pointers.

His meeting with Diaz goes down as one of the turning points in Renoir's career, to which must be added the revelation of Courbet and Manet. Everything points to an influence of Delacroix at this time, too, but his chief interest seems to have gone to Courbet first, then to Manet, who had just come into the limelight with an exhibition of modern painting at Martinet's, and again with the famous Salon des Refusés held in 1863. Manet's pictures, which had scandalized the public, made a deep impression both on the young group at Gleyre's studio and on several of their fellow students at the Académie Suisse, Pissarro, Cézanne and Guillaumin. Now, too, Renoir and Cézanne met and became friends.

Turned down at the 1864 Salon, but accepted in 1865 with his *Portrait of William Sisley* and *Summer Evening*, Renoir sent in to the 1866 Salon a canvas whose pigment was slapped on with the palette knife after the manner of Courbet—*Jules Le Cœur in Fontainebleau Forest*—but it was refused. Painted in much the same manner, his *Diana* was refused at the 1867 Salon. But Renoir soon realized that this technique was not for him, and, painting his *Lise with a Sunshade*, saw it accepted at the 1868 Salon. In the contrast of the dark belt against the white dress, we see the influence of Manet—an influence on Renoir that never went deep, however —as we see it again in the *Portrait of Alfred Sisley and his Wife*, with the red and yellow striped dress and the grey trousers. But though our first glance at the subject and composition brings Manet to mind, very different from him indeed are the well-rounded modeling of forms and the juxtaposed passages of light and shadow. Closer to Courbet is the *Bather with Griffon Terrier*, accepted at the 1870 Salon along with *Woman of Algiers*, an odalisque with reminders of Delacroix not only in the theme, but also in the color-scheme.

Portrait of Alfred Sisley and his Wife, 1868.

Lise with a Sunshade, 1867.

*Ice Skaters in the
Bois de Boulogne, 1868.*

La Grenouillère, 1868-1869.

16

It is a matter of considerable interest to see how different the land-scapes of the early paintings are from the figures. Their treatment—as we see in the *Park of Saint-Cloud* (1866) or the *Champs-Elysées* (1867) —is much more akin to Corot than to Courbet. In them, in fact, we find the first signs of Renoir's trend towards Impressionism, already discernible, moreover, in the *Park of Saint-Cloud* and the ice-skating scenes of 1868 and 1869, and patent in the views of *La Grenouillère*, which date from the same years. Of the three versions of the latter, those of the National Museum, Stockholm—painted from the same angle as Monet's *La Grenouillère*—and the Reinhart Collection, Winterthur, are a prelude to the boating scenes at Argenteuil after 1870, by virtue of the landscape reflected in the rippling water in distinctly separate brush-strokes. Suggested by the subject itself, this style it was, very probably, that led to the coining of a term—the famous "comma" brushstroke —that summed up impressionist technique.

Quite different, strangely enough, are the *Pont des Arts* (1868), a very neat, clean-cut piece of work, and *Lighters on the Seine*, a canvas in which, on close inspection, we can detect a skillful medley of Corot and Jongkind, two of the forerunners of Impressionism. But the subdued light and the cloudy sky *à la* Jongkind have nothing of the nimble, fluttering touch of an impressionist picture, while the very freely sche-matized treatment *à la* Corot bears no hint of the division of tones.

La Grenouillère, 1869.

A popular restaurant and bathing place on the Seine, a few miles downstream from Paris, near Bougival, La Grenouillère ("The Frog Pond") is referred to several times in the stories and novels of the Naturalist writers, notably in Maupassant, who describes it from his usual jaundiced point of view. Renoir, however, painted only the happy, carefree side of summer days spent boating and swimming there. Cool, crystal-clear light filters through the canvas in an all-pervading harmony of tender green and blue-grey, lit up here and there with a brighter dab.

The Goncourt brothers commented as follows in their Journal: *"Bougival, the landscape studio of the modern French school. Each bend in the river, each willow-tree, brings to mind an exhibition." Summering there in 1869, Monet produced this, his first thoroughly impressionist painting, for which he made countless preliminary sketches. It is more broadly, more powerfully scaled than Renoir's, but falls short of the latter's color harmony and unity of light effects. Fewer boats and fewer figures together with sparser foliage let a deeper breath of air into the picture, broaden the river and shift the stress on to the gleam and flicker of the rippling water.*

La Grenouillère, 1868.

The work of his predecessors had much to teach Renoir, but none of them can be said to have affected him decisively. Neither Courbet nor Manet left a lasting impress on his temperament, so different from theirs at bottom. As Renoir put it later on, he and his friends had looked to Manet "as the standard-bearer of the group, but only because his work was the first to get down to that simplicity we were all out to master." And so it seems in retrospect today. As against the sleek, insipid productions of the official painters, the work first of Courbet, then of Manet, must have seemed to these young men like an inspiring hope of salvation, with its directness, its disdain of any artifice, as fresh and clean as official art was bogged down with superannuated dogma. Even so, Manet had only been a stepping-stone; each of them was to go much farther along the path his own temperament dictated.

Claude Monet:
La Grenouillère, 1869.

Obviously inspired by Courbet, this canvas is Renoir's first full-scale study of light-and-shadow play amid leafage and rippling waters as it flickers over a figure and becomes the unifying principle of the entire composition. In a light summer dress and a dark hat, having shipped the oars and fallen to dreaming, a young woman languidly sits in a rowboat that has drifted against the grassy banks, beneath a tree whose overhanging branches gently skim the surface of the water and stir up glints of light. This canvas is an aggregate of lush, broad, unfused strokes, with dabs of red and light blue that "season" the dominant salad-green tonality.

The Boat, 1867.

*The Pont des Arts
and the Institut, Paris, 1868.*

The Franco-Prussian War of 1870 now scattered the group momentarily. Manet, Degas and Bazille volunteered or were called up, while Monet and Pissarro took refuge in England, as did Sisley, too, who was a British subject. Disregarding his calling-up orders, Cézanne slipped away to L'Estaque on the sly. Renoir, apparently shrugging his shoulders and leaving things to fate, politely turned down General Douay's offer of protection and found himself shipped off to Bordeaux, comfortably remote from the front. There he painted portraits of his company commander, Captain Darras, and his wife. After the capitulation, he spent two idyllic months of family life in a neighboring chateau, where he gave painting lessons to his friends' pretty daughter, was attended like a king, and spent his time horseback riding. His friends were reluctant to let him go for fear he would come to harm in the fighting that had broken out again. But he finally got away, and was soon dividing his time between Paris and his mother's house at Louveciennes, though in the hectic days of the Commune (March–May 1871) he ran considerable risk in doing so.

In later years he liked to reminisce about his experiences in these eventful days.

Lighters on the Seine, 1869.

20

Le Moulin de la Galette (detail), 1876.

Impressionism

As soon as life in Paris grew normal again, the young men drifted back, one by one, except for Bazille, who had been killed in the fighting at Beaune-la-Rolande. Soon the group was together again, toiling away and eager to see what the future held in store. Fully alive to the common ties that bound them, the Impressionists-to-be worked almost as a team. Manet had shown the way, but Monet now assumed the position of leader. The Argenteuil Period stood at hand, and Impressionism was about to take definitive form.

Determined to stand or fall by the "emotions of the eye," and ruthlessly doing away with all that might jeopardize a pure, forthright expression of them, these young painters tried to forget what they already knew about the things they painted, so as to record them in a fleeting moment of purely visual perception. Soon their eyes were opened to the startling changes of color as light changes; they saw that the old notion of local tones did not hold good, that values are inseparable from color, that outline drawing has no justification in nature but is a figment of the mind. Looking on the world with virgin eyes, they willfully reduced everything they saw to sensations of color, which they expressed in terms of small, juxtaposed dabs of pigment.

But these ideas were not hit on all of a sudden; they took shape slowly, following a distinct line of development. Renoir personally was always a little indifferent to the theories being debated around him, and we see him still following in the footsteps of Manet with his *Portrait of*

21

Portrait of Rapha Maître, 1871.

Rapha Maître (1871), in which his light and shade, though strongly clashing, attain none of the outspoken boldness and vigor of his elder. The shadow of Manet looms again behind the figures in his *Riding in the Bois de Boulogne* (1873), a large canvas posed for by the wife of Captain Darras, but weakened by shortcomings in the drawing of the horses. In 1872 he had painted his *Parisian Women dressed as Algerians*, almost a takeoff on Delacroix's *Algerian Women*. Renoir's picture, however, promises rather than achieves a harmony of its own, hampered as he was by the masterpiece that obviously inspired him.

Apart from the *Odalisque* of 1870 and this variation on the *Algerian Women*, only moderately successful, Delacroix's influence on Renoir is almost a craftsmanly one; it little affected his actual conception of the picture, its subject-matter or lay-out. The secrets he asked of the great Romantic were those of color and texture. Through Delacroix, as Claude Roger-Marx has shrewdly pointed out, Renoir made his way back to the all but forgotten strong points of Rubens and the Venetians. In this bent of his mind, characteristic even at this early stage, we have the essence of all that set him apart from the Impressionists. With his attachment to sculptural form and to modeling, its natural corollary, he delighted in smooth, rich, creamy textures with shot effects.

Riding in the Bois de Boulogne, 1873.

Odalisque or Woman of Algiers, 1870.

Although Delacroix's brand of romanticism and fondness for literary themes were not to his liking, Renoir, who always had a way of taking everything in his stride, never qualified his lifelong admiration for Delacroix, and particularly for the Algerian Women *(1834, Louvre, Paris)*, obviously in his mind when he painted these two pictures.

Parisian Women dressed as Algerians or The Harem, 1872.

Between 1872 and 1875, as had also been the case before 1870, Renoir painted his landscapes and open-air scenes in a technique often very different from that of his portraits and interiors. The move towards Impressionism, as might be expected, is much more obvious in the former works, though it is by no means steady-paced. No hint of it is visible in his *Quai Malaquais* (1872), for example, painted with a starkness of design in many ways reminiscent of Monet and, faintly, of Manet too. But full-fledged Impressionism is close at hand indeed in his *Pont-Neuf*, keyed in blue.

Claude Monet:
The Pont-Neuf, Paris, 1872.

The Pont-Neuf, Paris, 1872.

Though reminiscent of Corot and Lépine, this delicately handled view of Paris gives an unmistakable foretaste of Renoir's impressionist style, discernible in the discreet vibration of atmosphere and sunlight, and in the harmony of dark and light blues. There is no inkling, however, of the distinctly separate brushstrokes he was to take up the following year in painting The Duck Pond *in company with Claude Monet. Yet the two pictures strike a very similar note. At the Hôtel Drouot auction-sale in 1875, the* Pont-Neuf *was knocked down at 300 francs to a Monsieur Hazard, the highest price paid for a Renoir at the auction. At the Hazard Sale in 1910 the same picture fetched nearly 100,000 francs.*

Outright impressionist in its misty light effects, this picture was almost an act of faith in open-air painting, though at the very same period Renoir clung to traditional methods in his portraits and interiors. Taken in relation to the surprising range of quite different styles we find in his work in the ten years from 1870 to 1880, The Great Boulevards may be said to stand midway between a body of pictures painted in smooth, well-blended tracts of color and others treated as a patchwork of small, separate brushstrokes. What we have here, in fact, is a very subtle consolidation of the two techniques Renoir had been trying out —delicately blended brushwork that still produces a luminous effect of sparkle through blur.

The Quai Malaquais, Paris, 1872.

The Great Boulevards, Paris, 1875.

The Seine at Argenteuil, 1873-1874.

Regatta at Argenteuil, c. 1874.

The Duck Pond, 1873.

Claude Monet: The Duck Pond, 1873.

Monet painting in Renoir's Garden, c. 1875.

As they had done before 1870 with *La Grenouillère*, Renoir and Monet again, in 1873, made several sets of pictures on a common theme, this time *The Duck Pond* and the sailboat tied up on *The Seine at Argenteuil*. The first is painted entirely in thick, abbreviated brushstrokes, after the manner of Pissarro, the second in longer, more deliberate strokes. In each case the technique of both Monet and Renoir is the same.

Conspicuously absent from nearly all the landscapes of this period, the small isolated brushstroke reappears in Renoir's picture of *Monet painting in Renoir's Garden*. Usually he spread his color in thin layers, or smoothly blended his strokes into one another. As against this we have such serene, glistening scenes as the *Regatta at Argenteuil*, painted in about 1874, about the same time as similar pictures by Monet, though from a slightly different angle.

27

Dancer, 1874.

Portrait of Claude Monet, 1875.

Throughout his impressionist period—that is, from 1872 to 1883—Renoir practiced a disconcerting variety of techniques, putting on his color now in thick, squashing strokes, now in thin layers, now in distinct, separate touches, now in smooth strokes that melted into one another. Despite this versatility, however, the year 1875, with *The Great Boulevards*, may be taken as marking a peak in Renoir's development as an impressionist painter of outdoor scenes, though as yet he allowed no hint of this to creep into his other works. Take the small picture in the Louvre known as *The Rose* (1873) or *The Box at the Theater* (1874). Both of them remind us a little of Manet, but even more of Titian, Rubens and Watteau. Of all periods and none, quite timeless, they are simply great pictures. No stretch of the imagination can make them impressionist, either them or the little *Dancer*, with its creamily blended texture, no brushstrokes discernible, and the model's pose, so obviously that of a portrait. As for *The Box at the Theater*, only the subject is impressionist.

The Box at the Theater or The Loge, 1874.

It was not unusual for Renoir to switch from one technique to another in the same picture, as here, in the *Path winding up through Tall Grass, which we can date with reasonable certainty thanks to another country scene,* The Meadow, *very similar in style and treatment, and known to date from 1873. Only the foreground is painted in thick, vigorous, comma-like brush-strokes, while the middle distance and background glide away in thin, flat patches of color merging into one another. Renoir proves himself a master of his technical resources.*

The Meadow or
The Watering Trough, 1873.

Path in the Woods, 1874.

◁ *Path winding up through Tall Grass, c. 1874. Detail, pages 30-31.*

A Waitress at Duval's Restaurant, 1874.

Manet's presence is again felt in Renoir's portraits of the mid-1870s, all of them made outside the pale of Impressionism: *A Waitress at the Duval Restaurant, Alphonsine Fournaise*, even more in *Little Girl in a Pinafore*, and most of all in the *Portrait of Margot*. But even in the latter volumes are fuller and more softly rounded than Manet's.

We have to wait until 1876 to see Renoir painting portraits in small juxtaposed touches: the *Portrait of Victor Chocquet* with his hands clasped, *Mademoiselle Charpentier* seated, wearing blue, and above all the *Woman Reading*, her face a radiant source of light with its multitude of tiny touches running this way and that.

Mention of the names of Chocquet and Charpentier brings us to the subject of Renoir's intimates, the circle of friends, collectors and dealers that had now formed around him.

If the banner years of Impressionism fell between 1870 and 1880, this was due in the first place, of course, to a ripeness of style attained by the painters themselves. But in another sense it was brought about, too, by the united front they presented as a group, and by the common steps they took to gain recognition, with the backing of a few enlightened patrons, particularly their friend and fellow painter Gustave Caillebotte, one of the first to collect their pictures, and Paul Durand-

Woman Reading, 1876.

Young Woman in a Blue and Pink Bodice, 1875.

Ruel. This dealer had been a steady buyer of the works of the Barbizon painters. Then, in London in 1870, he met Pissarro, Sisley and Monet and took to their work at once. He bought and exhibited their canvases, but, put off by a sour welcome in Paris, he arranged for shows in London. It was only in 1873 that he met Renoir, who was later to say: "In 1873 an event took place in my life: I made the acquaintance of Durand-Ruel, the first picture-dealer, the only one for many long years, to have faith in me."

But despite a few sales in London, Durand-Ruel was soon running into debt, and was obliged to leave his young friends to their own devices for the time being. Abandoned by the one dealer who believed in them, outcasts from the official Salon, they rallied together and arranged for a show of their own. Their first group exhibition took place in 1874 in the studios of the photographer Nadar. Renoir showed six pictures: *Dancer*, *The Box at the Theater*, *La Parisienne*, *Harvesters*, a woman's head and a pastel *Sketch*. As all these works are in rather a traditional vein, Renoir fared best in the critics' vituperative accounts of the show, while Cézanne drew down a shower of abuse on his head. All the canvases of the new group were scathingly dubbed "impressionist" after the title of a picture by Monet called *Impression, Sunrise*.

Portrait of Victor Chocquet, 1876.

Portrait of Madame Chocquet in White, 1875.

Portrait of Alphonsine Fournaise, 1875.

Portrait of Margot, 1876-1878.

The exhibition attracted a lot of attention but made them a butt of ridicule more than anything else. So they decided against a similar show the following year. Instead, Monet, Renoir, Sisley and Berthe Morisot arranged for an auction-sale at the Hôtel Drouot, hoping to stir up some interest amongst buyers. This took place in March 1875 but was a complete fiasco. Exasperated cries of protest went up at each bid and the police were even called in to keep things in hand. Renoir put up nineteen paintings, which fetched a bare 2000 francs, most of which went to pay the expenses of the sale and to buy back several pictures that had gone for almost nothing. The best price he got was 300 francs for the *Pont-Neuf*, while the lowest was fifty francs for his *Woman walking in a Field*.

"Even so," he later told Vollard, "the sale had a happy ending for me, since I met Chocquet there. A modest employee in the customs, he had brought together an exceptionally fine collection. At that time, of course, and even considerably later, there was no need for a collector to be wealthy; good taste was enough. Chocquet had wandered into the Hôtel Drouot while our pictures were going up for auction. He was kind enough to find qualities in my work that reminded him of Delacroix, his idol. Writing to me the evening after the sale, he praised my painting to the skies and inquired if I would consent to make a portrait of Madame Chocquet. I accepted at once. As you know, I don't often turn down portrait commissions. If you have seen the portrait, Vollard, you must have noticed the copy of a Delacroix in the upper part of the picture. This was a work from Chocquet's own collection. He asked me to include it in the portrait. 'I want to have you together, you and Delacroix,' he said to me." In this *Portrait of Madame Chocquet in White* one can see behind her, on the wall, the Delacroix sketch for the ceiling decorations in the Palais Bourbon.

Nude in the Sun (Anna), c. 1876.

Anna, 1876.

Apart from the disheartening effect of the sale at the Hôtel Drouot, 1875 was a good year for Renoir. Commissioned to paint a group portrait for which he was handsomely paid, he was able to rent a small house with a garden. This he needed for the setting of his *Moulin de la Galette*, which he now embarked on with a small sketch made on the premises of the establishment. A typical *guinguette* of the period, an open-air dance-hall and café where the young people of Montmartre thronged for amusement on Sunday afternoons, the Moulin de la Galette, thanks to Renoir, has gone down as the symbol of those happy days, of the easy, carefree life in Paris in the late 19th century. His friends posed for him and he recruited their dancing partners from the milliners, seamstresses and flower girls who came to waltz at the Moulin in the evenings. Much of the *Moulin de la Galette* was painted on the spot, while in the garden of his house in the Rue Cortot he painted *The Swing* and the half-length portrait of *Anna (Nude in the Sun)*. These three works form a harmonious family of pictures, with their zones of shadow dappled with sunspots and leafage. One of the finest, most smiling of his masterpieces, the *Moulin de la Galette* is like a marvelous tissue of interwoven sunlight and soft, hazy blue. In it, forgoing the small separate touches he used for so many landscapes and open-air scenes at this period, he painted with crisscrossing brushstrokes, laid on in thin, successive layers and melting into one another, which respected form and volume, while at the same time rendering the luminous atmosphere bathing the figures.

Begun in 1875, the *Moulin de la Galette* seems not to have been completed until the following year. With Anna, the same model who had posed for *Nude in the Sun*, he painted another, very different picture now. Taking her in the cold light of the studio, he worked along traditional lines this time, but with a masterly freedom of touch that sets this nude beside those he painted twenty years later. These two studies of Anna seem to be the only nudes Renoir painted between 1870 and 1880. Yet, ten years later he had come to regard the nude as an indispensable art form; thirty years later he declared it to be the one essential art form. Why so few nudes before 1880 then? The explanation is the influence on him of Impressionism, far stronger, as we see, in his choice of sub-

Pages 40-41:
Le Moulin de la Galette
(detail), 1876. ▷

The Swing, 1876.

Bouquet before a Mirror, 1876.

Her First Outing, 1876.

ject-matter than in actual technique. For though he decked them out in a holiday air that lifted them above time and place, still he took his subjects from the life around him, and took just those themes that distinguish the Impressionists from all their contemporaries—sun-bathed landscapes, boating on the river, young people out-of-doors and so on.

About this time, too, he painted *Her First Outing*, a second *Box at the Theater*, though very different from the first, in which he sought to capture something of the atmosphere of the theater. To this end he

Portrait of Jeanne Samary, 1877.

Portrait of a Girl (La Pensée), 1877.

handled the two foreground figures and those in the background in sharply contrasting styles, the former delicately modeled, the latter indistinctly sketched in. Then he made a second portrait of Chocquet, no longer painted in small, separate dabs and dashes like the first, but in smoothly applied tracts of color, thick and even bumpy in places.

Still smarting from the disastrous auction-sale of the previous year, the friends reverted to the idea of a group exhibition in 1876 held this time at Durand-Ruel's gallery in the Rue Le Peletier. Renoir sent in a pastel and seventeen oils, six of them lent by Chocquet, amongst the others being the *Portrait of Bazille*, lent by Manet, *Little Girl in a Pinafore* and *Le Déjeuner chez Fournaise*. Reactions were, if anything, even more violent than before, and the press indulged in a field-day of derision and slander.

But another stroke of luck brought Renoir into contact with the publisher Charpentier, who commissioned portraits of his wife and children and became one of the artist's most loyal admirers. Though by no means a social climber, Renoir enjoyed mixing in society and never denied himself the pleasures of cheerful company and warm, human contact. Genuinely affable and easy-going, he was just as much at home in the simplest surroundings as in more cultivated circles. At the receptions held at the Charpentiers', he rubbed shoulders with the intellectual and artistic élite of Paris—Zola, Daudet, Flaubert, the Goncourts, Maupassant, Turgenev, Chabrier, Gambetta, Juliette Adam and Jeanne Samary, the actress whose portrait he made in 1877. This picture he sent in to the Third Group Exhibition that same year, together with twenty other canvases, including the *Moulin de la Galette*, *The Swing*, and portraits of Madame Charpentier, her little daughter, Mademoiselle Samary and Sisley.

Portrait of Victor Chocquet, 1876.

Madame Georges Charpentier and her Daughters, 1878.

Towards 1880 Renoir seemed on the verge of developing into a fashionable portrait-painter of women and children. He might well have seemed cut out for just such a role. A good mixer, never happier than when in stimulating company, he was equally at home in all circles of society. Though enjoying the simple things of life with gusto, he was also a connoisseur of refinement in all its forms. He delighted in the velvety, pink-and-white skin of women and children, the silky lightness of beautiful hair, the shimmering colors of fine robes graciously worn.

Renoir's wonderful gift for painting women's and children's portraits is shown at its best in this picture. Here we get the full-bodied savor of fine texture in painting, and all the grace and tenderness of childhood, without a trace of mannerism, despite the pose.

The impressionist way of seeing was far from being ideal for the limited field of the still life, in which the object is taken for itself alone. On the other hand, it is a perfect means of integrating generalized elements into a particular atmosphere. And in this fine portrait flowers, fruit and furniture cease to be merely inanimate objects, decorative accessories, or pictorial grace notes. Even when lying in the background, they enjoy their rightful share of the luminous, vibrant life of the picture as a whole.

The *Portrait of Jeanne Samary* may well be the most impressionist of Renoir's portraits. With no hint of shadow or darkness anywhere, with little or no variation in values, the whole canvas is a quilt of tiny, quivering touches, alive with light and a gemlike sparkle. In it Renoir dared everything in the way of mordant, acid-sharp colors, which he somehow integrated perfectly into that light whose secret was his alone. Also dating from 1877 are the *Portrait of a Girl*, sometimes known as *La Pensée*, and the *Portrait of Madame Henriot*—two misty, aerial works, the latter's texture as light as a veil—and his *Girl in a Boat*, whose composition harks back to Manet, with its brushstrokes jostling up against one another and respecting volumes, which here show marked differences in values and are built up in long, overlapping sheets of limpid color.

Not until 1878 did Renoir paint the large group portrait of *Madame Charpentier and her Daughters*. The period setting and the studied pose give the picture on the whole a conventional, rather worldly air that Renoir was soon to outgrow. But this need not prevent us from enjoying its many fine qualities.

His portraits of the Charpentier family and Jeanne Samary again opened the doors of the Salon to Renoir in 1879. He did not show with his friends at the group exhibition, either in 1879 or in the two years following. He now painted a new, full-length portrait of Jeanne Samary, but far less impressionist in technique than the first, and a small picture of *Two Little Circus Girls*. In the latter it is interesting to compare Renoir's approach with that of Degas and Lautrec. The latter both

Girl in a Boat, 1877.

Two Little Circus Girls, 1879.

Place Clichy, Paris, c. 1880.

48

Full-Length Portrait of Jeanne Samary, 1878.

At the Milliner's, c. 1876.

relished a harsh realism that, though often doing violence to the human body, completely captured the atmosphere of the circus. Renoir would have none of this. His models, far from being typical of the ring, are simply its youngest and most graceful performers, and he lovingly painted their youth and grace with no thought for the rest. The setting, probably added afterwards in the studio, is entirely secondary.

Standing apart in Renoir's work is *Place Clichy*, with its profile bust of a woman seen in close-up in the lower righthand corner. This unusual lay-out at once brings Degas to mind. The other portraits he painted at this time are quite devoid of effects of this kind. Witness those he made of Paul Bérard's daughters in 1879, Thérèse seen half-length and Marthe full-length. In the latter simplicity is the keynote; the model stands there as if patiently waiting for the click of a camera to leave her free to her own devices, while the flat colors are smoothly, neatly combined into a harmony of grey and blue. Equally casual and unstudied is the group portrait, made in 1880, of the Cahen d'Anvers children, two of them standing side by side, while the third is seated in profile, her

At the Concert or In the Box, 1880.

hands clasped in her lap, looking for all the world like a very good little
girl indeed. Also painted in 1880, but perhaps a little less stiff, the
portraits of the Grimpel children are just as charming, with one of the
girls in a blue ribbon, the other in a red one. Indifferent to innovations,
all Renoir sought for was the indefinable texture of women's skin, hair
and clothes, as together they subtly, delicately enhance one another, and
he achieved it as perhaps no one else has. Painted with a generous use
of pigment, sometimes almost over-painted, but always texturally rich
and satisfying, these portraits, even though the sitters are hardly more
than children, give off that scent of freshness and beauty in women that
Renoir alone can express, and which we welcome again in the picture
known as *At the Concert or In the Box*, dating from this same year.

Confiding, 1878.

The Garden in the Rue Cortot,
Montmartre, 1876.

It may well have been the open-air pictures painted in the summer
of 1876—*The Garden in the Rue Cortot, La Belle Saison, Conversation,* in
which figures are dissolved in a blaze of light—that led Renoir, in such
a canvas as *Confiding,* for example, to seek a certain homogeneity between the figures and the half-indistinct patterns that swirl behind
them, all painted in rich, well-blended colors. It is unusual, however,
for him to paint the human figure in the impressionist manner, which
completely volatilizes it. He almost always preferred a broader, unified
style, showing no qualms about the inevitable contrast it struck with the
small separate touches of the landscape. A good example of these two
distinct techniques is his *Woman with a Dog.*

Talking, 1879.

Woman with a Dog
(Aline Charigot), c. 1880.

Dead Pheasant in the Snow, 1879.

Woman with a Straw Hat
(Alphonsine Fournaise), c. 1880.

Woman Dozing, 1880.

Renoir spent the summers of 1879 and 1880 working out-of-doors on the Seine banks at Chatou and Croissy, and in Normandy at Berneval. He now painted his *Oarsmen at Chatou*, whose composition brings to mind that of Manet's *On the Banks of the Seine*, though their styles differ. Both artists build up the water in separate, lustrous bricks of color, the boat in broad tracts of unbroken color and the grass in elongated brushstrokes. But Renoir's texture, with its glazed effects of translucency, is altogether different, especially in the figures standing in the foreground.

At Berneval he began work on his large-scale *Girls fishing for Mussels*, a full-bodied, brightly colored painting. Then one of his friends, Paul Bérard, the diplomat, invited him to his home at Wargemont on the coast. Breaking away from the Seine banks, hitherto the single, unfailing source of inspiration for his landscapes, Renoir reveled there in new sights and scenery—new for him, though Monet had been happily painting on the Channel coast for years.

*Girls fishing for Mussels
at Berneval, 1879.*

Edouard Manet: On the Banks of the Seine, 1874.

Oarsmen at Chatou, 1879.

In the winter of 1880-1881 he finished off his large *Luncheon of the Boating Party*, a work probably sketched out in the summer of 1880 at Croissy, where he was staying with "la mère Fournaise." This is certainly one of Renoir's finest canvases. There are, however, several passages that may strike us as being a trifle dry. The light, on the other hand, is beyond all praise, playing beautifully over the young woman holding a puppy in the left foreground—none other than Aline Charigot, soon to become Renoir's wife—and the still life on the table, the leftovers of the picnic lunch. The girl in the center, lolling on the railing, outlined against the landscape, is again Renoir at his best. But we get a dissonant note in the lower righthand corner of the canvas, particularly in the man straddling the chair, with his hat pushed rakishly back, who is handled more dryly than the rest, and seen in a harsher light. Barring him, and the slight unbalance he creates, this is a well-nigh perfect picture of the glistening sunshine of a summer's day on the pleasant banks of the Seine. Similar effects of light filtering through an awning were experimented with in a smaller, more sketchy *Rowers' Lunch*.

Outings in the country around Paris and boating on the Seine were themes that never failed to inspire the impressionist painters. After the pleasure gardens of Montmartre, Renoir evoked the sunny, animated atmosphere of a riverside restaurant on the Seine in The Rowers' Lunch *(c. 1879) and, on a larger scale, in* The Luncheon of the Boating Party *(1881). Since his first pictures of La Grenouillère, done more than ten years before, Renoir had often painted at the nearby restaurant of Alphonse Fournaise, on the river island of Chatou, and that is the setting of this famous* Luncheon. *In it he rendered the peculiar effects of light filtering through a colored awning and memorably evoked the beauty of a summer's day out of doors. Nor did he ever succeed better than here in individualizing his figures, recording their distinctive movements and gestures.*

There are unmistakable differences of style, or simply of workmanship, in this picture. A little cold in places, the handling becomes more vibrant in others, most effectively in the still life of the boating party's well-laden table, in the young woman fondling the puppy, and also the woman holding her wine glass to her lips. Despite a textural opulence in many details worthy of the best Flemish masters, the fruit and bottles standing out on the white tablecloth are seen through a screen of atmospheric vibration set up by the gleaming dance of light as it impinges on objects, and by a slight blurring of color characteristic of Renoir's subtle brushwork. The young man straddling a chair, with a yellow straw hat, is the painter Gustave Caillebotte, a close friend of Renoir's, who built up a fine collection of impressionist paintings.

The Rowers' Lunch, c. 1879.

Boaters on the Seine at Bougival, 1881.

"*The boating party has had lunch under the awning of the restaurant. The picture was painted on the spot, in the open air. The Seine and its banks, lighted up by the summer sun, give it a glowing background... The men, while they would have been painted less well by another than they were by Renoir, might have had the same character that he has given them. But one cannot imagine these women, as they are here, having been painted by anybody else. They have the free and easy manners one would expect of young women who have lunched and are enjoying themselves with a group of young men, but they also have that graciousness, that roguish charm, which Renoir alone could give to women*" *(Théodore Duret,* Renoir, Paris, 1924).

The Luncheon of the Boating Party, 1881. Detail, pages 58-59.

Seated Nude, 1880.

Seated Bather, c. 1897. Etching.

Blue Nude, c. 1880.

Blonde Bather, 1881.

In the spring of 1881 Renoir went off on a six weeks' trip to Algeria, bringing back several landscapes with him. He spent the summer with the Bérards at Wargemont, then set out for Italy in the autumn. He took a great liking to Venice, with its misty golden light, and painted several pictures there, but for some reason Florence put him off, though he eagerly visited its museums, as well as those in Rome. He went to see the great Raphaels at the Vatican, and they surpassed his expectations and influenced all his subsequent work. Their effect, in fact, was almost immediate; we detect it in the features of the *Blonde Bather* painted at Naples only a few months later. He took in the ancient frescos at Pompeii, which delighted him, and then went over to Palermo with the idea of making a portrait of Wagner, who was just finishing *Parsifal*. But the composer, irritated at the intrusion, would grant no more than a half-hour of his time. Renoir took him at his word and in twenty-five minutes had painted his portrait, though the result was little to Wagner's liking, Renoir having taken with him the same liberties he would have taken with anyone else. It was now January 1882. He made his way back to France via Marseilles, stopping off to see Cézanne at L'Estaque, where the two friends painted together for several weeks. But unused to the treacherous climate, with its burning sun tempered by blasts of the mistral, Renoir came down with pneumonia. After getting back on his feet, he crossed to Algiers in March to convalesce.

Portrait of Richard Wagner, 1882.

Little Girl with a Blue Hat, 1881.

◁ *Algerian Landscape,*
Ravine of the Wild Woman, 1881.

Vesuvius, 1881.

Venice, St Mark's, 1881.

Venice, 1881.

Renoir, always responsive, always eager to satisfy his curiosity, felt intuitively that Venice would have much to offer him. And so he stopped there in the autumn of 1881 on his way to Florence and Rome. In Paris, shortly before, he had made the acquaintance of Whistler, who may well have told him about his own experience of the Venetian light in 1879-1880. Renoir himself experimented now with light effects—some of the subtlest in the whole of his work. The square of St. Mark's looms up as if through an autumn squall. On the Grand Canal the waters bristle with small broken waves, and rocking boats cut their way through the mist. Buildings are bathed in a snowy, all but colorless light. Renoir was delighted with Venice. Gazing at its pink and white marble, gilded by centuries of sunshine, he felt a sense of elation (whereas in Florence, a few weeks later, he was chilled by the black and white stonework of the buildings, too much like a check pattern for his taste), and he expressed it in a profusion of gay and spirited notations. Two of Renoir's Venetian paintings figured in the seventh group show of the Impressionists in 1882. And so, after Argenteuil and London, Venice entered the repertory of the new school.

Gondola in Venice, 1881.

Returning to Paris, he took part in the Seventh Group Exhibition of the Impressionists (1882), after having abstained for several years and showing only at the Salon. Now he sent in twenty-five canvases, a representative selection of his most recent work, including the *Luncheon of the Boating Party*.

The following year he painted three longish panels, inspired by couples dancing. One of them—*Dancing at Bougival*—harks back, both in spirit and treatment, to the recent scenes of boating and boaters, while the other two, *Dancing in the Country* and *Dancing in Town*, are almost outright decorations, on the whole rather stylized and, in some respects, hinting at the cold manner soon to come. The summer of 1883 Renoir spent in Guernsey, and wrote as follows to Durand-Ruel: "Here I am on a very fine beach, utterly unlike the Normandy beaches... We go bathing among the rocks, behind which we change, for want of anything better at hand. Nothing could be prettier than the sight of men and women huddled together on huge rocks. It's like stepping into a landscape of Watteau, rather than reality. This gives me a whole stock of lively, graceful themes on which to draw. Such delightful bathing suits! Here as in Athens the women haven't the slightest qualms about the presence of men-bathers beside them. What fun it is, slipping from

Dancing in the Country, 1883.

Dancing in Town, 1883.

boulder to boulder, to come upon the girls in the midst of changing their clothes. But even though English, they don't seem to mind. I hope to give you an idea of this delightful place, but I shan't have a great deal to show for my stay."

The beach scenes he brought back with him from Guernsey were painted in a new style, very much impressionist, with little difference in values and iridescent, clearly visible brushstrokes, but longer now and hugging the forms of objects, though never at the expense of freedom. Later on, after his "harsh" period, he reverted to a similar style, chiefly in some canvases painted at Essoyes, which also pointed the way to the long, sinuous brushstroke he developed after 1890.

Curious that on the eve of his reversion to line Renoir should have painted these Guernsey pictures in a style thoroughly impressionist, however different from Monet's brand of Impressionism. For while his brushstrokes here are neither particularly vibrant nor systematically separate and distinct, but elongated rather and pulling form together, they are still so free and flexible, so iridescent in their endless interplay in light, that they seem a very far cry from the things that were soon to preoccupy him. But then this was in the nature of a last fling at Impressionism before he gave it up for good.

As we see Renoir's impressionist period to a close, let us pause for a moment and examine the body of work that lay behind him now, almost bewildering in its diversity and difficult to classify. Never at any time was his an orderly, step-by-step evolution towards a fixed goal, but always a desultory growth, progressing by fits and starts, as likely to leap suddenly into the future as to slip back to a style he had practiced years before. We may thus expect to find different manners not only in different works of the same date, but also, on several occasions, in one and the same picture.

The real reason for this apparent fickleness is that Renoir followed no other guide but his own sensibility, which, though it made him a prey to every influence that chanced to come his way, never left him at the mercy of any particular one for long. However receptive to the lessons to be learnt from others, he remained impervious to hard-and-fast rules. The influence of his friends was undeniable, that of Monet in the early days being particularly obvious, but it was only sporadic and skin-deep. The same sensibility that left him open to Monet's style and technique when they worked together brought him safely back to his own resources as soon as he was alone.

Both his force and his weakness at the same time, Renoir's sensibility yielded him up to outside influence, but it as easily cast them off when they threatened to grow tyrannous. Though occasionally it led him to the brink of pitfalls, it somehow guided him safely away before it was too late.

Dancing at Bougival, 1883.

Study for Dancing at Bougival, 1883. Pen and ink.

Renoir turned thirty in 1871, forty in 1881, but even then, however experienced he had become, he cannot yet be said to have found himself.

Though many canvases, chiefly landscapes, prove him to be a skilled practitioner of the type of distinctly scattered brushstrokes used by Monet, these are not his greatest works. And though he had by now done some very fine figure paintings of women, their tremulous, ethereal style presented obvious dangers.

The best of Renoir went into the works that embodied the lessons of Impressionism without stiffening them into a rigid pattern, those, in other words, in which he integrated forms into light without breaking them up. Now these, in fact, were the very pictures in which he used a remarkably flexible technique, adapted to every peculiarity of the picture, rather than cut-and-dry methods reducing everything to a common denominator—the pictures, for the most part, in which he blended thin, limpid dabs of pigment smoothly into one another, and not those occasionally over-painted works with thick, disparate strokes of opaque color jostling one another.

"I painted two or three canvases with the palette knife, as Courbet was so fond of doing, and then I painted some with a full brush," he later reminisced. "A few of them came off, I suppose, but I found this a nuisance when I wanted to work them over again. I had to use a knife to pry away whatever I was dissatisfied with, and once I had put in a figure I couldn't move it without scraping the canvas. I tried painting in tiny dabs, which made it easier to run tones into one another, but then the surface is always so rough—that rather puts me off. Everyone has his likes and dislikes. I like to fondle a picture, run my hand across it. But damn it all, when they're painted like that, I feel more inclined to strike a match on them. Then there's the dust that settles in the crevices and mars the tones."

With his keen feeling for the atmospheric light playing over people and things, it was only natural for Renoir to embrace Impressionism. But the trail blazed by Monet was not his own. And this, together with his spirit of independence, was the essential factor in his finally breaking away from a movement to which, though in sympathy with it, he had never blindly adhered, as the diversity of his work at this time proves.

L'Estaque, 1882.

The Umbrellas, 1882-1883.

The Harsh Period

A S WE HAVE seen, Renoir's independent turn of mind kept him always a little on his guard against Impressionism, and thus prevented him from indiscriminately assimilating a technique that, like all techniques, was neither infallible nor a panacea for the problems of painting. But by 1884 a vague sense of dissatisfaction had ripened into an open revolt against all his previous work.

What he had seen of Raphael at the Farnesina and the Vatican had left him a little uneasy, as had the sight of the ancient frescos at Pompeii. Shortly afterwards, when he happened to read Cennino Cennini's treatise on painting, he felt increasingly dissatisfied with himself. But whatever the effect of these chance encounters, in themselves they are not enough to account for the changes that came over his work. The important thing is that they found him at a sufficiently advanced stage for the new departure they induced him to make.

The impressionist way of seeing, almost wholly concerned with fleeting atmospheric effects, had never suited Renoir, whose feeling for form was not to be repressed. So we find him falling back hard on form now, but with a rigor and coldness that were just as alien to his temperament as the hazily melting lines of Impressionism had been.

The Umbrellas, painted about 1883 or perhaps even slightly earlier, is a transition work. Although we cannot help feeling a measure of harshness here and there, most noticeable in the left foreground figure and the umbrellas, at the same time much else owes an unmistakable

71

Les Grandes Baigneuses (The Large Bathers), 1887.

Nude Study for The Large Bathers,
1884-1885. Pastel and wash. ▷

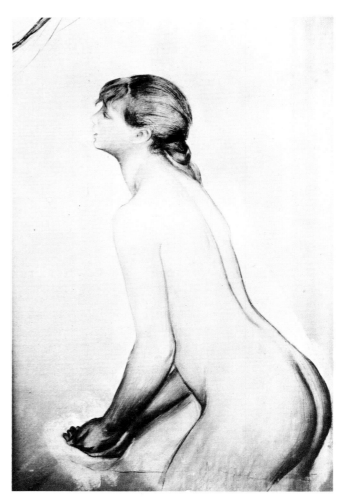

François Girardon:
Nymphs Bathing, late 17th century. Bas-relief, detail.

debt to Impressionism. The entire right-hand group, for example, with the two children and the fondly smiling woman beside them, is quite devoid of any coldness.

Taking inspiration, it seems, from a bas-relief by Girardon at Versailles, in 1883 or 1884 Renoir went to work on his *Grandes Baigneuses*, on which he spent two hard years. Choosing as he did a classical subject unconnected with any time or place, he freed himself of any well-defined aesthetic program and set technical recipes. The reappearance of the nude, almost entirely absent from his work in the years between 1870 and 1880, heralded the new phase he was entering. His methods of work, furthermore, he now completely overhauled.

To begin with, he primed his canvas with a thin coat of white lead, spreading it with the palette knife over the colorman's surface preparation, so as to secure a flawlessly smooth ground on which to work. Intent on a taut, close-fitting design, he drew and traced his motifs over and over again, tightening, firming up and correcting them until he got exactly the lines he wanted, which he then meticulously traced on to the canvas. So doing, he made preparatory drawings in charcoal, red chalk and blacklead pencil, media he had hardly explored hitherto. He applied his colors with great care, avoiding a solid impasto now in favor of a very thin, smooth, enamel-like layer of pigment in complete contrast with the impressionist technique, and reminiscent of painting on porcelain, even of fresco painting. All the while he kept to the lowliest tones of his palette: red and yellow ochre, terra verde, cobalt blue, black. Out of these methods arose a new style, in the great decorative tradition, certainly with something of Boucher about it, of his *Bath of Diana* most of all, the picture that had been Renoir's first great love.

The Large Bathers, 1885-1902.

The Children's Afternoon at Wargemont, 1884.

Portrait of Lucie Bérard, 1884.

Though he had set to work on it in 1883-1884, *Les Grandes Baigneuses* was not completed until 1887. In the meantime he produced a number of works whose treatment varies—the impasto of some is even fairly thick and the surface rough to the touch—but all of which have this in common: pure, clean-cut contours and a strict pruning away of non-essentials.

The Children's Afternoon at Wargemont (The Bérard Children), painted in 1884, exemplifies his new manner in all its coldness and uncompromising severity. Impossible, as we look at the picture, not to muse on all it might have been, had Renoir let himself go instead of practicing this austerity. There was some justification for his self-denial in *Les Grandes Baigneuses*, verging as it does on outright decoration, but here there is none. The atmosphere of a country house on a sunny, midsummer afternoon was a theme that begged to be treated with the warm serenity and gladness of heart Renoir had lavished on the *Moulin de la Galette* and the *Luncheon of the Boating Party*. As it is, the elements of the picture are coldly locked together, all life largely wrung out of them, and we can only imagine the harmonies he would have woven them into a few years before.

In the Jardin du Luxembourg, 1883.

Bather combing her Hair, 1885.

Woman plaiting her Hair (Suzanne Valadon), 1886.

1. *Motherhood, 1885.*
2. *Motherhood, 1886.*
3. *Motherhood, 1886.*

The *Portrait of Lucie Bérard* (1884), formerly in the Gangnat Collection, shows a face drawn with the stark cast a Primitive painter might resort to. In 1885, when his son Pierre was born, Renoir painted his young wife suckling the baby, an accurately drawn picture whose colors have all the soft limpidity of a painting on porcelain. He twice reverted to this theme in 1886, with a few changes in the background and the color-scheme, the first version keyed in yellow, the second in a shade of violet obtained by the pink of the jacket striking into the blue skirt and the blue of the skirt striking into the pink jacket. In 1918 Renoir made a final, smaller version of this picture.

In other canvases, such as the *Bather combing her Hair*, the pigment is put on—much as Cézanne put it on in his still lifes—in closely mingled touches that modulate color and, continually superimposed on one another, form a rich, thick texture contrasting with the coldly accurate linework.

In 1886 he painted *Woman plaiting her Hair*, a canvas sufficiently reminiscent of Ingres to warrant the usual practice of describing this phase of Renoir's career as Ingresque. (The model for this picture was Suzanne Valadon, the mother of Utrillo, who also posed in 1883 for *Dancing in Town* and *Dancing at Bougival*.)

Girls playing Shuttlecock, 1887.

Girl with Cow and Ewe, 1887.

Portrait of Marie Durand-Ruel, 1888.

The peak of the Harsh Period came in 1887 with his *Girl with a Cow and a Ewe* and *Girls playing Shuttlecock*. The figures in both are dry and cold to a degree no other work by Renoir can rival. Yet the landscape backgrounds of both are thoroughly impressionist, clashing badly with the stiff, very clean-cut lines of the girls and animals. The landscape behind the girls amusing themselves at shuttlecock, exceptionally fine, makes this anomalous mixing of styles even more regrettable. But Renoir was not blind to these excesses, and having reached their culmination here, and having served to work old habits out of his system,

Girl with her Cat
(Portrait of Julie Manet), 1887.

they led him to a fresh point of departure. The crisis had passed, and passed very quickly, as is plain to see from his *Girl with her Cat* and the *Blonde Bather*, both painted in this same year, 1887.

In the *Girl with her Cat*, a portrait of Julie Manet, only the face is still treated in the Ingresque manner. The rest of the picture is wonderfully free and full-bodied, while the linework is anything but cold or cramped. Even so, the model, though only a child at the time, was much intrigued by the way Renoir went about his work, and she has related how he first thinned his colors, laid them on the canvas patch by patch, and after each sitting stowed the canvas away in a damp corner of the cellar to keep the colors from drying. Now these methods were still those of his Harsh Period, for later on he customarily began by covering the entire canvas with a light scumble. As for the *Blonde Bather*, though the face tends to be stylized much as that of Julie Manet, the rest of the picture is handled even more freely; the whole lower half, in fact, is only broadly sketched in.

The *Daughters of Catulle Mendès at the Piano* bears out this trend, for though fragments here and there are still a little cold, faces stylized and attitudes rather stiff, the general atmosphere vibrates with life.

The Daughters of Catulle Mendès at the Piano, 1888.

Little Girl in a Park, 1883.

La Coiffure, 1888.

Sometimes a vestige of coldness is betrayed no longer by the rigid precision of outlines, but by a rather artificial pose and the acidity of the tones, for example in *La Coiffure*, in which a woman in green, standing up, combs the hair of a woman in pink seated on a red plush chair. Elsewhere, as in the *Young Woman Bathing*, standing up to her hips in the water, the porcelain-like sheen of the nude body harks back to the Harsh Period, despite the easy freedom of the linework. Again, only the heavily stressed contours of a work like the *Bather Drying Herself*, with its creamy richness of texture, warns us not to date it from ten years later. Every picture he painted in 1888 shows Renoir drawing a little freer of the formulas that had hampered him.

Still it would be misleading to think that, during these critical years of transition, he held his warm and expansive nature completely in check. Several works prove that he did not, particularly the *Seated Bather* (1885), as well as several landscapes, a subject inimical to excessive starkness of treatment—which accounts for his having painted so few of them in this period.

Young Woman Bathing, 1888.

Bather Drying Herself, 1888.

Seated Bather, 1885. Pencil heightened with gouache.

Blonde Bather, 1887.

It is not known for certain whether the small, very misty sketch of *The Harbor at La Rochelle* (also painted by Corot) actually dates from the trip Renoir made there in 1884, or from 1895, as Julius Meier-Graefe maintains. The picture itself, at any rate, can hardly be described as cold, but then it may have been the memory of Corot that kept him out of danger. Renoir spent the early summer of 1885 at La Roche-Guyon, then moved to Wargemont and then to Essoyes, his wife's home, where from now on he spent part of nearly every year. But no landscapes painted at this time have been positively identified, nor have any painted the following year, when he stayed at La Roche-Guyon, then at Saint-Briac in Brittany. We learn from his letters that he was painting hard, but the work he refers to must have been nudes of bathers or other outdoor scenes, and not landscapes. There is one outdoor scene, however, that may be regarded as a landscape, such scant attention having been paid the figures. This is *The Bench in the Garden*, which Meier-Graefe assigns to 1886. It is frankly "harsh" in its precision, the outlines of each leaf being plainly visible to the eye. And there are other landscapes like this one, apparently made when the spirit took him, the leaves of the trees meticulously outlined one by one in Indian ink. Renoir resorted to pen and ink in a number of watercolors dating from this period.

The landscapes painted on the banks of the Seine in the summer of 1888 are quite different. Despite their very distinct brushstrokes, however, they betray a faint starkness and lack of air of which no inkling was ever to be found in the pictures painted prior to this period. But these scars were soon to heal.

A picture of the *Montagne Sainte-Victoire*, dated 1889, is proof that Renoir again paid a visit in that year to Aix-en-Provence, after having stayed with Cézanne at the Jas de Bouffan the previous winter before going to Martigues. For this landscape, dotted with full-blown trees, was obviously painted at the height of summer. As we examine his handling of the theme, so different on the whole from anything by Cézanne, we cannot fail to be struck by the geometrical form of the mountain, as Renoir saw it, which thus shows the extent to which Cézanne's geometry is genuinely that of nature herself.

Sailboats at Cagnes, c. 1888.

Seated Bather drying her Foot, c. 1890. Red, white and black chalk.

The Iridescent Period

THE impressionist way of seeing, with its emphasis on fleeting atmospheric effects, sorted badly with Renoir's temperament and his natural love of sculptural form. But the cold manner he adopted in reaction to it was equally ill-suited to one so deeply enamored of light as he was. And it was only after he had thrown off the shackles to which he had voluntarily submitted that his true nature broke through again. It was then but a step to the mature style of his middle and final years, the style that fully reconciled the opposite poles of his previous work. From now until his death he painted those magnificent nudes bathing not in water, but in the light of another world.

Many of the pictures dating from about 1890—but not all by any means—are still transitional works. Not quite compatible with the style that lay just ahead, they are tokens, rather, of an evolution that had still to come full circle. In them, however, though the harsh manner has gone by the board entirely, there is a perceptible groping for a new brand of Impressionism, one very different from that of ten years before. Far from being a reversion to old loves, this was a step into the future for which the experience of the Harsh Period had paved the way. Renoir had realized that cold linear contours were not for him, and had given them up. But what he did not give up were the strong forms they had contained, and from now on these were the backbone of his work.

We get a good idea of this mutation of style if we examine, for example, his *Apple Vendor* (1890). Of all the pictures he painted now, this is the most impressionist, both in technique and in the effect it produces, and proclaims its kinship with the works he brought back from Guernsey in 1883. What we have is a group of women and children out-of-doors, in a clearing under trees, speckled with patches of sunlight and shadow—the whole thing painted in thick, plainly visible strokes of the brush. But strokes which, instead of sundering them, hug forms, build them up and model them, while the more smoothly blended brushstrokes of the *Moulin de la Galette* were merely content to respect forms, and those of his really impressionist pictures broke them up outright. This, then, is the fundamental difference between Renoir's impressionist period and his post-1890 work.

Several scenes of peasant life, probably painted at Essoyes, are handled in much the same style. In the other, less impressionist works of this period, even more attention is paid to modeling and this was the trend of the years to come, with the broader, freer brushing that led to the flickering, elongated strokes of his maturest canvases. The tendency to mold form, which we detected in the Guernsey pictures, had grown to a full-fledged technique, with the outlines of old having fallen away for good. Renoir modeled forms now in their mass and their light, his touches jostling one another, running together or blending completely, as the case might be. Hair, flesh, landscape backgrounds—none were treated in quite the same manner. This has been called his Iridescent Period, characterized as it is by glowing, pearly colors and a mellow, creamy-soft texture.

Bather, 1893.

Bather seated on a Rock, 1892.

This picture brings out the difference of style between the Harsh and the Iridescent Periods, on the one hand, and Renoir's Impressionist Period on the other. No longer bound by the outlines that previously set them off, forms now are modeled by a tide of elongated, freely flowing brushstrokes that wash up against them, shaping and building them, whereas the impressionist brushstroke all too often dissolved and volatilized form. This was Renoir's solution to the conflict of form versus light—a technique enabling him both to build form and to integrate it into the atmospheric light.

Bather tying up her Hair, 1892-1895.

Chosen among many examples, the *Bather tying up her Hair* and the *Bather seated on a Rock* are typical of the new vein in which he was working in the 'nineties, as are many pictures of girls in summer dresses. Their hair, either flowing loosely or bunched in the shadow of their beribboned, broad-brimmed hats, is usually handled in the same manner as the green and leafy backgrounds into which they so harmoniously merge, in the sunlight flooding in from above. *Girls by the Sea* shows this style at its best.

Yvonne and Christine Lerolle at the Piano, c. 1890-1898.

◁ *Girls at the Piano, 1892.*
◁ *Girls at the Piano, 1892.*

Girl Reading, 1892-1895.

In a few paintings, which may be considered transitional works—
though, chronologically speaking, they are not—, he reverted to the
textural meagerness and acrid colors of the 'eighties, e.g. *Girls at the
Piano* and *In the Meadow*, thin, bodiless paintings that are more like
miniatures on ivory or decorations on porcelain. And though their
linework is neither hard nor cold, but well wedded to forms, still they
have none of the glowing opulence of the works we have just discussed.

The *Girl Reading* and *Nude Asleep* are two of the finest interiors he
painted between 1890 and 1900. And though, now as later, a painter of
the female nude before all else, Renoir still found time for landscapes.
It was no longer the chosen theme of his impressionist years, but he still
worked hard at it, for reasons of his own, whenever he had opportunity
to do so during his holidays in the country and at the seaside.

Besides his almost yearly visits to Essoyes, he stayed with Berthe
Morisot at Mézy in 1890 and 1891. He seems to have brought back no
pictures with him either from his stay in the South of France in the
winter of 1891 or from his trip to Spain with Gallimard the following
winter, no doubt too busily engaged in making the rounds of the museums and feasting his eyes on Velázquez, El Greco, and especially
Goya, whom he found greatly to his liking.

The summer of 1892 he spent in Brittany, whence he wrote to
Berthe Morisot: "I have ended up at Pornic, where I'm teaching my boy
to swim. All's well in that quarter, but I've got to get down to some
landscapes. The country here is nice, and that puts me in a great rage
with myself. I find landscapes more and more of an ordeal, especially as
I feel dutybound to do them. It's the only way to keep one's hand in
practice. But to take up my stand out there like a performing showman,
I can hardly stomach that any more."

In the Meadow or Gathering Flowers, 1890.   *The Apple Vendor, 1890.*

But however sharp his distaste for the work—an attitude that sets him well apart from Monet, Pissarro and Sisley, each a born landscape painter—he produced several views of Pornic in a soft, woolly style. And though he added: "I went over to Noirmoutier, a superb spot quite like the Midi, much superior to Jersey and Guernsey, but much too far away," he seems to have made a stay there all the same, if we judge from a letter Berthe Morisot wrote to Mallarmé shortly afterwards: "I saw Renoir at the funeral of the poor little Durand boy (Charles Durand-Ruel). He had just come in from Noirmoutier and meant to go back the next day. His wife and son are having a fine time at the beach."

He spent the winter of 1892-1893 in the South of France, writing from Saint-Chamas to Berthe Morisot: "I have thought much of you, wondering if you wouldn't like to see the most beautiful spot in the world. This is it. Here you get Italy, Greece and the Batignolles quarter of Paris all wrapped into one—plus the sea."

The summer of 1893 saw him first at Pont-Aven in Brittany, then with the Gallimards at Benerville, near Deauville. But he wrote: "I didn't stay long at Benerville. Though it has its charm, I can't say I care much for this stretch of Normandy. So I'm leaving the big-name places behind me to see the Normandy we are unfamiliar with."

In 1894 his friend Caillebotte died. Renoir had been named executor of the will and throughout the following winter this involved him in endless bickering with the Beaux-Arts officials, who flatly refused to accept the pictures Caillebotte had left to the Louvre. Renoir only partially succeeded in overcoming their resistance.

In the summer of 1894 he revisited the Gallimards in Normandy, then went to Essoyes, returning to Paris in September for the birth of his second son, Jean.

Girls by the Sea, 1894.

*The Bay of
Douarnenez,
Brittany, c. 1895.*

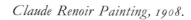
Claude Renoir Painting, 1908.

Claude Renoir Playing, c. 1906.

Berthe Morisot and her Daughter Julie, 1894. Pastel.

The Artist's Family, 1896.

In January 1895 he left for the south, staying at Carry-le-Rouet with his young pupil Jeanne Baudot and her parents at the home of friends of theirs, the Jourdes. He urged Berthe Morisot to come and join them, repeatedly sending her detailed directions for the trip. But she was delayed by the illness of her daughter, bed-ridden with a bad case of influenza, which she in turn came down with, and when congestion of the lungs set in she died in early March. Renoir, who had always been very close to Berthe Morisot, hastened back to Paris at once.

The following summer, accompanied by Berthe Morisot's daughter Julie, now an orphan, his wife and two sons, Pierre and Jean, he spent the holidays in Brittany, first at Pont-Aven, then at Douarnenez. The landscapes he made there have all the easy brushwork and vigorous colors of his later painting.

The Road from Versailles to Louveciennes and *The Essoyes Road*, both painted in a warm, blurred technique, also date from 1895, as do—very probably—the two views of Montmartre as seen from the old house where he was then living, known as the Château des Brouillards. In the background of one of these we can make out the scaffoldings of the Sacré-Cœur, then in the process of construction. Dating from 1896 is the large canvas of *The Artist's Family*, in which we see Pierre in a

Gabrielle and Jean, c. 1895.

Two Heads of Coco, c. 1903.

sailor's suit hanging on his mother's arm, Gabrielle kneeling down to steady Jean, and on the right the young daughter of Paul Alexis, who lived next door to Renoir at the Château des Brouillards.

Many times between 1895 and 1900 Renoir painted his second son Jean, as a chubby-cheeked baby playing with his toys in the arms of Gabrielle in 1895, as a tot of three, as a little boy with a ribbon in his long hair in 1899, then sewing, puzzling over the alphabet, holding his hoop in his hand. He showed himself as incomparable a painter of children as he was of women, and he went even farther along this path after 1900 with the many portraits of Coco, his third son.

At Essoyes in the summer of 1897, while learning to ride a bicycle at the direction of Abel Faivre, the caricaturist, Renoir fell and broke his arm. In 1898, to please his wife, he rented a cottage at Berneval, but he no longer cared for the Normandy coast and described the cliffs as "absurd lacework." None of the pictures he painted there are seascapes, but all views of the countryside, very silken and smoothly blurred in treatment. The same smoothly blended texture recurs in the landscapes painted at Essoyes, where he now bought a house, as it does in those painted at Cagnes, in the foothills behind Cannes, where he spent the winter of 1899-1900, only to settle down there for good in 1903, after making brief stays nearby at Magagnosc and Le Cannet.

Doctor's orders now obliged him to make his home on the Mediterranean. For no sooner had he reached the height of his powers and fame, and freed himself at last from financial worries, than his health was suddenly crippled by arthritis. He had felt it coming on for several years, with an occasional twinge on sodden winter days and at the seaside in summer. But a severe attack in December 1898 laid him low, and from then on, little by little, the joints of his arms and legs stiffened until, after 1911, he was confined to a wheel-chair, though he never ceased to paint.

Even before illness curtailed his activities, he had become something of a stay-at-home, painting and enjoying his family to his heart's content, the vagabond, sociable years of his youth far behind him now. Still, throughout the last years of his life, living in seclusion at Cagnes on the Riviera, he paid a visit every summer to Essoyes and to Paris, places he loved and could not do without.

Two Women in a Garden, 1895. Pastel.

Woman Reading, c. 1895.

Bather drying her Leg, 1905.

Fulfillment at Cagnes

No gap can be said to exist between the bathers of the Iridescent Period and those subsequently painted at Cagnes. Each is a member of the same family, though the latter, like all the late work, show his increasing delight in sculptural form.

This new trend naturally led to a stronger emphasis on modeling, and the colors of forms were shaded off, not to say blurred, by freely flowing strokes of the brush melting into one another more completely than they ever had before.

This style is a far cry from anything we found in the so-called Harsh Period, when Renoir, fearing to see everything solid and durable in painting slip irretrievably from his grasp amidst the flashing lights and colors of Impressionism, had resolved to secure forms beneath a taut network of contour lines. But this strictly linear containment of them never came natural to him; it was a check on his true temperament. And casting about in the late 'eighties for the technique that would reconcile form and light, to the detriment of neither, he found it at last when he discarded stiff outlines and let masses expand in terms of the light playing over them. At the same time he found the style that, all things considered, suited him best.

From now on he got the satisfaction of starting out with firmly grounded volumes and working up progressively to the finished picture. He began by priming his canvas with a light scumble on which he laid in his masses. This was the first step. The second consisted in

Nude Asleep, 1897.

Woman and Child in a Garden, 1903.

Three Bathers, c. 1897.

Though the easy freedom with which he handled them links these bathers to the Iridescent Period, the softened-off modeling is a foretaste of the great post-1900 bathers of Renoir's old age. They prove, furthermore, that there was no hiatus between the earlier and later bathers. Another version of this work exists, in which the three women, become almost baroque, are even more freely handled than here, and in which the brushstrokes are longer and more distinct. The version reproduced here may be a little later in date, which would account for the slight differences in treatment.

modeling the masses, working them into shape by burnishing the facets that caught the light and deepening the color of those that remained in shadow. The third and final operation was to lay in the accents and highlights that set their tone and gave life to forms.

Albert André, who knew Renoir well, has left an account of the way he produced these jewels of light and color: "His early training as a painter on porcelain left him with a lifelong fondness for bright, translucent colors. Today the white ground of his canvas has taken the place of the chinaware of old... When the subject is a simple one, he goes at his picture first by brushing in a few very sketchy guide lines, usually in red-brown, so as to proportion the elements that will make up his

Graziella, 1910.

picture, the 'volumes,' as he slyly calls them... Then, without a pause, he takes pure tones diluted with turpentine, much as if he were painting in watercolors, and rapidly spreads them over the canvas, until you see indefinite, iridescent shapes appearing, with all the tones running into one another, shapes that delight your eye even before you can make out what they are.

"At the next session, when the turpentine has had time to evaporate, he goes to work on this undercoat, proceeding in much the same way, but with a little more coloring matter in the oil and turpentine now. To brighten the parts that are meant to face the light, he applies pure white directly on the canvas. He deepens shadows and half-tints in the same way, directly on the canvas. He does no mixing, or almost none, on the palette itself, which is covered with tiny, oily, comma-like dabs of almost pure tones. Little by little he gets his forms into shape, but always letting them mingle with one another. 'I want them to kiss,' as he puts it.

"A few more brushstrokes... and rising out of the color haze of the first state you see softly rounded forms, glistening like precious stones, and wrapped in golden, translucent shadows."

Unlike Manet, who went straight to work with a hard, flat, square-shaped brush, dripping with color, Renoir laid in his colors on the original scumble gradually, with a round, flexible, tapering brush, applying them in thin, transparent layers, one above the other, each veiling the last without concealing it. In this way he obtained a smooth, silky, lustrous texture, full of deep, limpid gleams, very much in the tradition of the Venetians, Rubens and Watteau. It should be made clear, however, that such a technique is quite the reverse of that which consists in veiling a coarse, plainly visible undercoat with a glazing. He disapproved of this procedure and blamed Degas for having induced a pupil to use it, declaring: "I consider an art inferior when there's a secret behind it. Nothing is hidden in the paintings of Rubens and Velázquez. Those who ramble on about glazing don't know what they're talking about. They're looking for trade secrets that never existed, and don't exist in that picture Degas had young Rouart copy."

The work he referred to is Mantegna's *Virtue victorious over the Vices*, which Degas had set his pupil to copying, having him prime the canvas with an apple-green grounding on which a glaze was then applied. Renoir began a picture in the opposite way, with a low-pitched, lightly

The Judgment of Paris, 1908.

Bather pushing back her Hair, 1905-1906.

blurred scumbling, which he then covered over with the highlights and accents that brought forms and colors to life.

Renoir's technique remained essentially the same from the Iridescent Period to the end of his life, but as he grew older he practiced it with increasing freedom and mastery. His palette, largely reduced to earthy colors and cobalt blue during the Harsh Period, now blossomed out again, composed of the following tones: red lake, vermilion, red-brown, yellow ochre, Naples yellow, emerald green, cobalt green, terra verde, cobalt blue, white and ivory black. For several years before and after 1905, he worked ivory black into the modeling of flesh-parts, whose color thereby took on a leaden hue. When he gave up this practice, his nudes regained all the luminosity and blandness of tone that characterized them up to the end.

Outstanding examples of this shaded-off modeling, to which the admixture of ivory black gives a murky cast, are the *Bather drying her Leg* in the São Paolo Museum, and the *Bather pushing back her Hair* in the Belvedere, Vienna.

As against these, the *Two Bathers* in the National Museum, Stockholm, and the series of *Bathers* and *Odalisques*, as well as the large *Nymphs* in the Louvre, bathers and nudes painted after 1910, show even more delicate, limpid modeling, within a red-golden color-scheme.

Here Renoir attains that gorgeousness which has led to his being likened to the Venetian masters of the Cinquecento. All the coruscating brilliance of his palette is called into play, reaching an unexampled pitch of chromatic intensity. Breaking with the impressionist principle that blacks should always be rendered by blues, he uses for the first time some ivory-black in Gabrielle's hair. Her figure compactly fills the full space of the canvas, following a layout in which Renoir particularly excelled.

Seated Nude, 1916-1917.

And in them, form may truly be said to issue from the colors themselves, rich and luscious as it is, like fully ripened fruit.

Now, whether he painted landscapes or still lifes, washerwomen, bathers, nymphs, odalisques or allegorical figures, nude or dressed in bright-colored garments, Renoir made them of the same clay, with the same hand, lovingly building them up round radiant points of light, which he took as so many interchangeable cores to be fashioned into flowers, fruit and women's bodies.

Bathers represent by far the major part of his late work. But all these magnificent creatures, bathers, odalisques or washerwomen, are at one with every other element of the picture. Anxious not to sunder human beings from their surroundings, Renoir continued for the most part to paint them in luxuriant landscapes. And these, whether taken in their own right or merely regarded as a background, are ever more richly, more lyrically colored, while the way in which they are built up in terms of basic volumes is more or less apparent according as they are left in the rough or highly finished.

Gabrielle before a Mirror with Flowers and Jewelry, 1910.

These monumental bathers are a characteristic example of the final Cagnes period, with their wholly spatial conception of form as opposed to the linear conception that had preoccupied him during the Harsh Period. Here we can detect each element of the picture taking its rise as a simple volume, then blossoming out to its optimum fullness of form, sustained by highlights and accents of color. The absence of outlines and the full-bodied modeling enabled Renoir to work every part of the picture into a flawless whole—an achievement crowned by the perfect harmony in which the women coalesce with the landscape setting.

Two Bathers, c. 1915.

Though often they are left in a blurred, indistinct, rudimentary state, or merely touched up with a few highlights, at other times we find these masses transformed into lakes of fire, aglow beneath a lusty barrage of accents, which, as time went on, were more and more intensely colored, more and more full-bodied. Licking up like tongues of flame, they now became increasingly vivid and red. And red, in fact, was the dominant color of Renoir's last works, though on occasion, as in the *Garden at Les Collettes* (also known as the *Blue Landscape*), it gave way to harmonies of intense blue-greens.

Stripping away all but essentials, he took no thought now for carefully arranged bouquets and still lifes, preferring fruit, flowers or fish against the simple backdrop of a white tablecloth. He painted them as he painted his figures and landscapes, in terms of volumes fashioned round kernels of light and overlaid with accents of color. The best and richest of Renoir's last years is concentrated in the roses, peaches and berries that cluster along the edge of some of his canvases, though many times, too, he painted them separately, taking deep delight in doing so.

The fact is that we can trace Renoir's development from start to finish in the field of the still life alone. In his *Arum and Hothouse Plants* of 1864 the contrast of light and shadow, while not carried to the lengths to which Manet carried it, is still a plainly intended one. Typical of the 1870-1880 years, *Bouquet before a Mirror* shows the impressionist breaking-up of form. We find the object again intact in the Harsh Period, but isolated from the rest of the picture. Fully integrated into the atmosphere in the Iridescent Period, it finally takes on the value of an absolute in the works painted at Cagnes.

"His painting," wrote Albert André, "is one of the few, when we take any part of it, to give us the same intense pleasure we get from a fragment of a fresco or a stained-glass window, a bit of silk, or a piece of sculpture. No square inch of any picture but embodies all the charm, all the inventions of his brush."

So it is that now, in any fragment of these late paintings of flowers, fruit and women's bodies, we get a concentrate of the glowing colors and textural richness that, in former years, had gone to ends at once more varied and more limited in scope.

As before he had sacrificed incidentals to essentials, so now he moved on from the particular to the general. He began to ignore the individuality of his models and to take them as so many universal patterns of form and color. The portraits he painted from this time on all belong to the same family, and to the same generation, while the light in which his bathers revel is the immutable summertime of a different world, remote from that whose subtle atmosphere hung over the banks of the Seine.

Reclining Nude, 1914.

The treetrunk in the middle, standing out sharply against the shrill white wall of the house, introduces a strange note in the picture, every other part of which is obviously built up strictly in terms of the masses. In fact the trees and shrubs on the righthand side have largely been left in the rough, with no effort made to bring out highlights and accents. Such is not the case in other landscapes painted at Cagnes, in which accents take on a vigor and intensity that may vary here and there, but which never openly clash or disturb the overall harmony of the composition.

Bathers, odalisques or washerwomen, whether nude or decked out in bright colors—all, for Renoir, are inseparable from the trees, flowers or fruit around them, whose being is intimately connected with their own. Elements of one world, each takes its rise as an indefinable mass slowly built up round a point of light, which Renoir takes as its center of gravity, and which he spins out into its final accents of color. Carried several stages further than in the Garden at Les Collettes, this landscape subtly hints at the underlying masses behind the accents of color that give them life and form.

*View of Montmartre, with the Sacré-Cœur
Basilica under Construction, c. 1895-1900.*

108

Pages 110-111:
Bathers, c. 1918-1919. ▷

Washerwomen at Cagnes, 1913.

This gorgeous sublimation of a Provençal scene is a good example of those "polychromatic symphonies" which so much delighted Renoir in the work of Delacroix. Here the painter avails himself of every color on his palette, but not to demonstrate its range, nor for a mere display of virtuosity. What he achieves is a carnival of light, a miracle of brilliant translucency. All the tones dear to Renoir meet and clash and join in a counterpoint of color that baffles description, yet has an immediate appeal. Each group of figures could make a separate picture; yet, so well and classically are they balanced and linked together, that no part can be suppressed without impairing the unity of the whole.

Like the aging Cézanne painting at the Bibemus quarry near Aix, Renoir at Cagnes seemed in search of the original foundations of the visual world. But while the first sought this structure in a geometrical cosmos of colored planes, Renoir approached it through spheroid formations of volumes. And while Cézanne's final efforts left him restless and dissatisfied, Renoir's filled him with a deep sense of well-being and serenity.

Before the many paths that lay open to him, he pondered long and deeply. But as he reached the threshold of maturity he made his choice, and though it is still an object of controversy, he found it, for him, the right one. And the way he chose to go led him to a fulfillment of his creative powers such as few artists have experienced.

He painted joyfully up to the very end, and died at Cagnes on December 3, 1919, at the age of 78, leaving behind him a monumental body of work.

Self-Portrait with a White Hat, 1910.

The River Scamander, c. 1900. Etching.

The Message of Renoir

WE have seen how in the course of his long career Renoir cast an interested eye on many contemporary masters, Diaz first, then Corot, Courbet, Manet, Delacroix and Monet. But in trying to understand the full significance of his achievement we do best to disregard its manysidedness, which a strictly analytical approach is apt to overstress, and to view it, rather, in its entirety. Then we see the underlying unity of all his works, painted at different times, in different styles, and we feel the guiding mind behind their ever-changing aspects.

Though he tried his hand at various techniques, some of which suited him, while others did not, he never ceased to be himself. At only one point do we have anything like a break in the continuity of his art: the anxious years of his Harsh Period. But this was only a break from the technical point of view; it concerned specific pictorial problems, not the artist himself. All the ventures in which his open-mindedness, his freedom from any preconceived ideas, involved him were for Renoir so many fruitful sources of discovery.

Diaz—whose paintings, as Renoir lamented in later years, "have ended up so dark, though when they were made they gleamed like precious stones"—taught him to shun dark painting and dingy colors in general, though fortunately he remained unaffected by the lingering traces of Romanticism in that artist's work. While caring little for Courbet's literary and didactic realism, Renoir took to heart the example he set of keeping in close touch with real life, and it was only after testing

113

it out in several pictures that he decided that Courbet's method of painting with the palette knife was not for him. From Corot, with whom, more than with any other artist, he was temperamentally akin, he learnt the value of a direct, unsophisticated approach to nature, followed by a careful revision in the studio of work done out-of-doors. Manet taught him the lesson of visual truth, but he was never able to accept Manet's reduction of ocular experience to the two extremes of light and shadow, nor his omission of all those intermediate shadings that he, Renoir, particularly relished. He liked Monet's way of seeing because it was less schematic, more diffused, more vibrant than Manet's; it was in keeping with his own temperament. But he did not restrict himself to separate-stroke brushwork, which tended to volatilize form. He preferred the vibrancy to be got by intense light and by the blending of one tone into another with translucent touches that soften transitions, rather than by the juxtaposition of opaque dabs of pigment.

He found this fusing of tones by translucent touches in Delacroix, to start with (to whose oriental and romantic side, however, he gave a wide berth), then in the Venetians, Rubens and also Watteau, the artist to whom he probably owed most.

"It's in the museums that one learns to paint," he once observed, but added: "When I say that an artist learns to paint in the Louvre, I don't mean that he wears his eyes out poring over old canvases and filching the master's tricks, only to do Rubens or Raphael all over again. His painting has got to be contemporary. But it's in the museums that he acquires the taste for painting that nature alone can never give. It isn't a pretty view that makes one want to be a painter, it's a picture."

Beyond the art currents and schools that come and go, Renoir links up with the great traditions of painting. Had he been born in the days of Titian, or Rubens, or Watteau, we may feel sure he would still have been the same Renoir, though then he might have found a climate more propitious than the late 19th century. He could have dispensed with Impressionism, which had merely an adventitious interest for him. The same is true of all the various art movements of his period: Romanticism, Realism, Naturalism, Impressionism and, slightly later, Symbolism, Fauvism, Cubism and Expressionism. All these were only so many side-issues for an artist like Renoir, whose temperament and gifts set him apart. He only spoke his mind when he said: "Painters fancy themselves extraordinary creatures. If once they take it into their heads to put on blue instead of black, they imagine they are going to change the face of the world. Personally I have always refused to set up as a revolutionary. I have always felt, and still feel, that I am simply carrying on what others have done before me, and done much better than I."

This healthy skepticism towards anything at all resembling progress or revolution in art proves that Renoir, who all his life made a point of learning things for himself, never had any illusions about the distance he had covered. Not that he steeped himself in false modesty; few artists have ever been more completely themselves. If he adopted techniques closely akin to those that had been the stand-bys of former masters, he did so not out of a reactionary bias, but simply because, after trying many, he found these more congenial than others. "When I was a beginner," he said, "I put on my green and yellow very thickly, in the belief that I was getting stronger values. Then one day I noticed that, with a light scumble, Rubens outdid all my impasto."

Renoir's great lesson lies in the utter integrity, warm-heartedness and simplicity of the man. Hardly a lesson anyone can learn, however, as it demands superb peace of mind existing above and beyond inner conflicts and cross-purposes. His psychic constitution was a godsend to Renoir; his good humor and love of life never flagged, even through the trials of his final illness.

Keen-witted, open-minded, overflowing with affability and good will, Renoir moved easily with people and enjoyed the things around him. And just as in art an equal success attended all his efforts—whether painting on porcelain, painting fans or even blinds, and every possible genre of easel painting—, in the same way he took equal pleasure in mixing with people from all levels of society. He liked simplicity in those around him, but he could single out and appreciate the most refined minds, and was equally at home with both. An innocent where class distinctions were concerned, he recognized only one class: the human family. Fame and wealth, for Renoir, were words at which he smiled. The only wealth he knew was that of his own nature, which he put unstintingly into his painting—the warm, human expression of all the joy he took in simply being alive.

From the *Park of Saint-Cloud* of 1866 up to the *Nymphs* of 1918, by way of *La Grenouillère*, *Le Moulin de la Galette*, *The Luncheon of the Boating Party* and all the bathers, pearly-skinned and iridescent, his painting is a song of delight in the beauty of the world and the sweetness of life. Whether he painted children, women, flowers, fruit or landscapes, the song was the same, and its triumphant note resounds in the harmony he achieved between the human being and the atmosphere and surroundings in which it moved. "I struggle with my figures until they are one with the landscape in which they stand," he said, always intent on fusing tones in light, on harmonizing the different elements of his picture. Thus he was led to mingle tones with one another, either by means of separate touches or smoothly blended brushwork.

An ambition already realized in one sense in the *Moulin de la Galette* (1876), as it was in another in the *Two Bathers* at Stockholm (c. 1915), this fusion of figures and things in light attains its paroxysm in the Cagnes landscapes, where it throbs with a cosmic vibration.

His world of harmony and light is a world in which original sin has yet to occur. Renoir was as free as a man can be of the guilt complex that has clouded the modern spirit. Having never set foot in Hell or seen an ogre, he let such things be. He was neither possessed of dark passions to work off or anguished obsessions to unburden on others. He was, in a word, a free man—free to exult in a landscape, a flower, a fruit, a face, a body golden in the sun, free to express their beauty and communicate it joyfully in terms of his art.

La volupté de peindre—so he described it at the far end of his life. Fifty years earlier, in his student days at the Ecole des Beaux-Arts, he had replied in the same spirit, with all the ingenuous freshness and spontaneity of his nature, when the professor, with a disapproving glance at his work, observed sarcastically: "You no doubt paint merely to amuse yourself."—"I certainly do. If painting didn't amuse me, I can assure you I wouldn't be here doing it."

This anecdote was recorded by Albert André, who added: "All Renoir is in this reply to Gleyre. He painted because it gave him intense pleasure to do so. He was never one to believe that by spreading his colors over the canvas he thereby performed a sacred rite, or, as he laughingly put it himself, that he was saving the Republic."

His healthy outlook on things is like a breath of fresh air in an age like ours, when so many are out to divorce art from any pleasure-giving sensation. Renoir never made a secret of what he thought: "To my mind, a picture should be something agreeable, cheerful and—yes!—nice to look at. There are too many nasty things in the world as it is, without our adding to them. I know that few people are prepared to admit that a painting can really be first-class and cheerful at the same time. Because Fragonard knew how to laugh, he was dismissed as a second-rate painter. People who laugh are never taken seriously."

And he concluded, with a smile: "Art in a stuffed shirt, whether painting, music or literature, will always go over."

Renoir returning from a painting expedition at Le Cannet, on the Riviera, 1901. Photographs.

Drawings, Prints and Sculptures

Unquestionably Renoir is not only a great painter but a great drafts-
man... As his work unfolds and develops, one finds that the changes in his
manner of drawing always run parallel to changes in his manner of painting,
and one sees too how easily he found the right means of recording his under-
standing of forms.
He had the knack of catching children's movements in rapid sketches.
He set down in flawless lines the pure forms of bathers. He caressed with
tenderness the young flesh of newborn babes. He made you feel the weight of
a woman's breasts, the full curves of her legs and arms. Without passing
judgment he saw through to the soul of his sitters, and saw it without asperity
or blackness.

Albert André, Renoir, *Paris, 1919*

Renoir stated towards the end of his life that he had never let a day
go by without painting unless prevented by force majeure. It should be
added that wherever he went, on a journey or for a walk, and in the
different studios he occupied, he always kept his sketchbook close to
hand. However, he set no great store on his sketches and a great many
of them have been lost or destroyed. During his lifetime he only exhibited a few portraits in pastel. The first exhibition devoted entirely to
Renoir's drawings was not held until 1921, two years after his death; it
comprised an impressive collection of one hundred and fifty pastels,
watercolors, drawings in charcoal and red chalk. The few studies still
extant in pen and ink or lead pencil that were too closely related to the
paintings of his early youth were excluded from the show.

Like the other painters of his group, Renoir did hardly any drawings during his purely Impressionist phase, though he peopled his dancing sunlight with human figures. In 1879 the Paris publisher Georges
Charpentier, with whose social circle he mingled, launched a weekly
magazine entitled *La Vie Moderne*. This led Renoir to draw a number
of illustrations of literary texts and portraits of celebrities, some of
which he later repeated in pastel.

Renoir reacted intensely to the general crisis in the Impressionist
group that coincided with Manet's death. "About 1883," he told Vollard later, "a sort of break occurred in my work. I had got to the end
of Impressionism and had reached the conclusion that I could neither
paint nor draw. In a word, I was in a blind alley."

It was not until after his trip to Italy (1881-1882) that line occupied
a truly important place in Renoir's work and was responsible for a
turning point in his artistic development. In 1883 he took the Dance as
the subject for several paintings for which Suzanne Valadon was the

model. The pen drawing representing the central couple in the famous picture, *Dancing at Bougival*, was used as an illustration for a short story by Paul Chote, *Mademoiselle Zélia*. From this story comes the inscription on the drawing: "She waltzed with delightful abandon in the arms of a fair-haired man who looked as if he went in for boating."

The brief phase that has been called Ingresque, which followed his trip to Italy, marks a searching effort to recapture at its source the purity of form that had been dissolved by a too exclusive cult of light. A great many preliminary studies in pencil sometimes heightened with red or white chalk led to the large-scale composition entitled *Les Grandes Baigneuses*, which is one of the highest peaks of French classical art between Jean Goujon and Matisse. The largest and most complete of these studies, a pencil drawing heightened with red and white chalk, marks the culmination of Renoir's Ingresque period.

There would be no explaining the artist's final blossoming, which combined with such mastery volumes and lights, the pictorial fluency of the Venetians and the plastic majesty of Antiquity, without the linear discipline he sought so intently and consistently at a decisive turning point in his career. In an endeavor to conjure up the myth of Venus and glorify woman's physical beauty, which for him was the very life-breath of the visible world and the forces of nature, he succeeded in achieving with the red chalk inherited from Boucher and Fragonard a new, heightened power of suggestion. The forms burst forth from within in all their luminous fullness, no longer outlined by an arabesque but, as Elie Faure said, "enveloped by a musical murmur."

The motif of the female bather, either standing or seated, illustrates the transition in Renoir's work from the Ingresque manner, best characterized in pencil drawings, to the supple, broad manner that found its perfect expression in red chalk. Towards the end of his life, his inborn feeling for the Mediterranean tradition and his love for the female form as the universal symbol of nature inspired a number of mythological compositions. The most important is *The Judgment of Paris*, which he executed three times in painting and once in sculpture. The large drawing in red chalk heightened with white chalk is a study for the first version painted in 1908. The painter's maid Gabrielle, who was his favorite model at the time, posed for the figure of Aphrodite and also for the shepherd Paris, who kneels before her wearing a Phrygian cap and offers her the apple that was the prize for the fairest of the fair.

When his fingers were so paralyzed by rheumatism that they could not even hold a stick of all too brittle chalk, charcoal or crayon, he used a paint-brush to sketch on his canvas a few strokes that blossomed at once into colors. "If one could have taken some canvases out of his hands at the very moment when drawing was on the point of giving way to color," says his confidant, Albert André, "what precious buds one might have preserved and how they would have broadened the sense of the word drawing!"

"Just look at Renoir's nudes, that is sculpture for you!" exclaimed Maillol.

Renoir only took up sculpture late in life, when crippled with rheumatism, and for most of them the actual execution was done under his supervision by Richard Guino, a pupil of Maillol recommended to him by Ambroise Vollard. Guino proved himself to be not only a faithful and reliable executant, but a highly sensitive interpreter of Renoir's ideas and intentions. So much so that these works have been rightly described as the fruit of a close collaboration between "mind and hand."

All of them bear the unmistakable mark of Renoir's plastic genius. In many he showed his power of recreating from lowly models the classic goddesses of legend well able to vie with their majestic sisters of Antiquity and the Renaissance.

The Milliner, c. 1879. Pencil.

Dancing in the Country, 1890. Etching.

Dancing Couple. Drawing.

Scene from Zola's L'Assommoir, *c. 1877-1878. Pen and bistre.*

Young Woman with Muff. Pastel.

Venus, frontispiece for Mallarmé's Pages, *1890. Etching.*

Two Bathers, 1895. Etching.

Three sketches on the theme of Motherhood, after 1885. Lithograph.

Mother and Child, 1916. Bronze.

Pierre Renoir, front view, 1893. Lithograph.

Medallion Portrait of a Woman, 1918. Drawing.

Woman picking Fruit. Watercolor.

Portrait of Pierre Renoir, c. 1890. Drawing.

Seated Nude. Drawing.

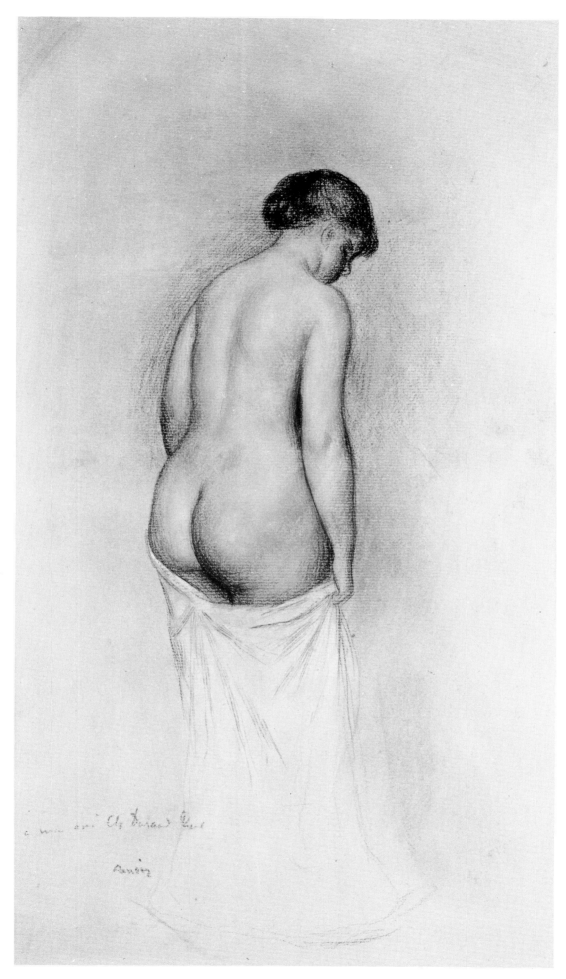

Nude with Drapery, 1884. Red and black chalk.

Study for The Bathers, 1884-1885.

Bather, 1895. Red chalk.

The Judgment of Paris, 1908-1910. Red and white chalk.

The Judgment of Paris, 1914. Bronze.

Medallion of Coco, c. 1908. Plaster.

Bust of Madame Renoir, 1916. Bronze.

Bust of Claude Renoir (Coco), 1908. Bronze.

Washerwoman, c. 1916. Bronze.

Washerwoman, 1917. Bronze.

Blacksmith, c. 1916. Bronze.

Venus Victorious, side view, 1914. Bronze.

Dancer with Tambourine, 1918. Plaster.

Pipe Player, 1918. Plaster.

Biography and Background

1841 Birth at Limoges, February 25, of Pierre-Auguste Renoir, son of a small tailor. The family numbered seven children, two of whom died young.

> 1839 Birth of Cézanne and Sisley.
> 1840 Birth of Monet.
> 1841 Birth of Frédéric Bazille and Berthe Morisot.

1845 The Renoirs move to Paris, settling in the Carrousel quarter.

> 1848 Birth of Gauguin.
> 1853 Birth of Van Gogh.

1854 Renoir begins his apprenticeship as a painter on porcelain.

1858 Seeing his profession threatened by newly invented processes of mechanical reproduction, he gives up painting on porcelain. To earn a living, he paints fans, then decorates blinds.

1862 Gives this up in turn, now that he has saved enough money to keep him going for a while. Follows courses at the Ecole des Beaux-Arts, Paris, and enrolls in Gleyre's studio, where he meets Monet, Sisley, and Bazille.

> 1863 The Exhibition of Modern Painting at the Martinet Gallery and the first (and only) Salon des Refusés open the young men's eyes to Manet's painting. In the summer they work together out-of-doors at Chailly-en-Bière in the Forest of Fontainebleau.
> Death of Delacroix.

1864 While painting in the Forest of Fontainebleau, Renoir makes the acquaintance of the Barbizon painter Diaz.

1866 A stay at Marlotte, near Fontainebleau, where he paints "At the Inn of Mother Anthony." His entries are rejected at the Salon.

1867 His "Diana" is rejected at the Salon. Shares Bazille's studio.

> 1867 Death of Ingres. Birth of Bonnard.
> Paris World's Fair.

1868 His "Lise" is accepted at the Salon.

1869 Renoir and Monet work together at Bougival, where they paint "La Grenouillère," a bathing spot on the Seine.

1870 His "Bather with Griffon Terrier" and an odalisque are accepted at the Salon. During the Franco-Prussian War, he serves at Bordeaux in a light cavalry regiment.

> 1870 "The Batignolles Studio" by Fantin-Latour.
> Bazille killed in action.

1871 Renoir returns to Paris during the Commune.

1872 Studio in the Rue Notre-Dame-des-Champs. "Le Pont-Neuf."

1873 Meets the dealer Paul Durand-Ruel. Studio in the Rue Saint-Georges. Paints with Monet at Argenteuil on the banks of the Seine.

1874 First Group Exhibition of the Impressionists. "Box at the Theater." Meets the painter and collector Gustave Caillebotte. Both Renoir and Monet paint "Sailboats at Argenteuil." Death of his father.

1875 Auction-sale at the Hôtel Drouot with Monet, Sisley, Berthe Morisot. Meets the collector Victor Chocquet. "The Great Boulevards."

1875 Death of Corot.

1876 Second Group Exhibition of the Impressionists. Meets the publisher Georges Charpentier. Two portraits of Chocquet, "Le Moulin de la Galette."

1877 Third Group Exhibition. "Portrait of Jeanne Samary."

1877 Death of Courbet.

1878 "Madame Charpentier and her Daughters."

1878 Théodore Duret publishes "Les peintres impressionnistes," the first serious study of the Impressionists.

1879 Accepted at the Salon with his portraits of Jeanne Samary and Madame Charpentier, Renoir takes no part in the Fourth Group Exhibition. Meets the diplomat Paul Bérard, who invites him for the summer to his home at Wargemont, near Berneval on the Channel coast.

1880 Stays at Chatou, an island in the Seine near Bougival, at an inn run by "la mère Fournaise," where he begins "The Luncheon of the Boating Party," for which his wife-to-be, Aline Charigot, is one of the models.

1881 Travels to Algeria in the spring, and stays at Wargemont with the Bérards during the summer. Leaves for Italy in the autumn, visiting Venice, Florence, Rome, Naples, Pompeii.

1882 Palermo: "Portrait of Wagner." On the way back he visits Cézanne at L'Estaque, where he catches pneumonia. Convalesces at Algiers. Seventh Group Exhibition, at which Renoir shows 25 works.

1883 One-man show in April, arranged by Durand-Ruel; Duret prefaces the catalogue. Summer in Guernsey. A trip with Monet in December from Marseilles to Genoa; they visit Cézanne at L'Estaque. Reads Cennino Cennini's 15th-century treatise on painting. "The Umbrellas."

1883 Death of Manet.

1884 Breaks with Impressionism and reverts to line, entering his so-called Harsh Period. Begins "Les Grandes Baigneuses." Summer trip to La Rochelle, where Corot had painted.

1885 Birth of his first son, Pierre. Summer stays at Wargemont, then at La Roche-Guyon with Cézanne. Autumn at Essoyes, in the Champagne country, his wife's home.

1886 Successful Impressionist Exhibition in New York, organized by Durand-Ruel.

1888 End of Renoir's Harsh Period. Stays with Cézanne at the Jas de Bouffan, then at Martigues in the winter. In December his face is partially paralyzed.

1889 Revisits Cézanne, then stays at Montbriand, near Aix.

1889 Paris World's Fair.

1890 Forgoing emphatic linework, Renoir adopts the freer, richer style that characterizes his Iridescent Period. Studio at 11, Boulevard de Clichy, Paris. Three-week stay in the summer with Berthe Morisot at Mézy, on the lower Seine west of Paris.

1890 Death of Van Gogh.

1891 Trip in the winter to Tamaris, then to Lavandou, on the Riviera. Short stay at Mézy in the summer.

1892 Trip to Spain with Gallimard. One-man show at Durand-Ruel's; sells his first picture to the State. Summer stays in Brittany, at Pont-Aven, Pornic, Noirmoutiers.

1893 Winter at Beaulieu. Summer at Pont-Aven, then at Benerville with the Gallimards.

1893 Opening of the Vollard Gallery, Paris.

1894 Death of Caillebotte, who leaves his collection of impressionist pictures to the State. But Renoir, his executor, only succeeds in having a part of them accepted. Another summer stay with the Gallimards, then at Essoyes. Birth of his second son, Jean. Lives in an old house in Montmartre known as the Château des Brouillards. Studio in the Rue Tourlaque.

1895 Staying in the South of France, he returns to Paris at the news of Berthe Morisot's death. Summer in Brittany, at Pont-Aven, then at Tréboul on the Bay of Douarnenez. Also works at Louveciennes, near Paris.

1896 Death of his mother. His enthusiasm for Wagner wanes after a trip to Bayreuth. Lives in the Rue de la Rochefoucauld, Paris. Exhibits at Durand-Ruel's.

1897 Summer at Berneval on the Channel coast, then at Essoyes (Champagne), where he breaks his arm.

1898 Stays at Berneval, then at Essoyes, where he buys a house. First severe attack of arthritis in December.

1899 Winter at Cagnes, near Cannes. Rents a house at Saint-Cloud, near Paris, for the summer, then takes a cure at Aix-les-Bains.

1899 Death of Sisley.

1900 Winter at Magagnosc, near Grasse. Summer at Louveciennes and Essoyes. Takes part in the large-scale art exhibition at the Paris World's Fair.

1901 Winter at Magagnosc. Birth of his third son, Claude, nicknamed Coco. Another course of treatment for his arthritis at Aix-les-Bains.

1902 Settles on the Riviera at Le Cannet, near Cannes.

1903 Winter at Le Cannet, then he moves back to Cagnes, living in the Maison de la Poste. Summer at Essoyes.

1903 Founding of the Salon d'Automne in Paris.

1904 Course of treatment at Bourbonne-les-Bains. Retrospective Exhibition of Renoir's work at the Salon d'Automne.

1905-1909 His arthritis grows worse. Settles for good at Cagnes, where he buys a plot of ground known as "Les Collettes" and builds a house. Visits Essoyes and Paris each summer.

1906 Death of Cézanne.

1910 His health taking a turn for the better, he makes a trip to Munich.

1912 Partially paralyzed and confined to a wheel chair, he paints with the brush strapped to his hand.

1914-1915 His two sons Pierre and Jean are both badly wounded early in the war. Death of Madame Renoir.

1919 After summering at Essoyes, he visits the Louvre in his wheel chair, where he watches the hanging of his own "Portrait of Madame Charpentier" and sees Veronese's "Marriage at Cana," thus fulfilling a long-felt desire. He died at Cagnes on December 3.

Renoir's studio at Cagnes, 1917. Photograph.

Renoir in his house at Cagnes, on the Riviera, 1917. Photograph.

List of Illustrations

Works are listed in chronological order.
Dimensions are given in inches, height preceding width.

RENOIR: OIL PAINTINGS

155

SKIRA

FILMSETTING, PHOTOLITHOGRAPHY AND PRINTING BY
IRL IMPRIMERIES RÉUNIES LAUSANNE S.A.

Acknowledgements

Color photographs are from the Skira Archives, except for those supplied by the Museum of Fine Arts, Boston (page 69), the Réunion des Musées Nationaux, Paris (pages 30-31, 40-41, 110-111), and the National Gallery of Art, Washington (page 13). Black and white photographs are from the Skira Archives and the Lionello Venturi Archives, except for those supplied by the Barnes Foundation, Merion, Pennsylvania (pages 56, 90, 93), Bulloz, Paris (pages 22, 72, 145), François Daulte, Lausanne (page 74), Giraudon, Paris (pages 10, 12, 32, 36, 44, 61, 79, 80, 122, 130), Lauros-Giraudon, Paris (pages 126, 129, 139, 140, 141, 146, 147), Paul Mellon, Upperville, Virginia (page 119), Réunion des Musées Nationaux, Paris (pages 10, 64, 68, 132, 144), Roger-Viollet, Paris (pages 23, 81, 120, 127, 128, 142, 143, 152) and Sammlung Oskar Reinhart, Winterthur (page 18).